# The
# Lemonade
# Stand

Michelle Faust
Lemonade Legend
www.lemonadelegend.com/the-lemonade-stand

Publisher's Cataloging-in-Publication data
Faust, Michelle et. al.
The Lemonade Stand / Michelle Faust
Edited by Casanova, Corrine
1. The main category of the book —Memoir.
2. Another subject category —Leadership.
3. More categories —Overcoming Obstacles.

FIRST EDITION

# Contents

# Foreword

## by Karen Nowicki

*H*eart Word: Forgiveness / "When we forgive others, we give ourselves permission to heal, and to no longer be chained to the past. Forgiveness is the threshold for an inspired future."

Short bangs and pigtails, the 9-year-old me is happy. She loves putting on performances in the back yard with friends, playing kickball in the street, and selling lemonade for 25 cents on the sidewalk in front of our house. Sure, a skinned knee or a sibling argument here and there. But overall, life is easy and free.

With high school behind her, 19-year-old me is finding her way through her first year of college and balancing a checkbook. When a check bounces, she calls dad, and he puts more money in the bank with a reminder that, at some point, she'll need to budget better and manage this on her own. Boyfriends, study groups, and football games — life as an "almost adult" person is still uncomplicated. She's traded in her Dixie Cup of lemonade for a Long Island iced tea in a red Solo cup.

Now, with her firstborn in her arms, 29-year-old me is working full time as an assistant principal by day and pursuing her master's degree by night. She's feeling overwhelmed and is estranged from her husband. She breaks down crying when she hears a commercial about postpartum depression, realizing she needs professional help. She no longer fits in her hot pink bikini with the bright yellow lemon pattern sprawled across the matching top and bottom.

The years continue as they do for all of us. At 39, she is blindly in a relationship that puts addiction, infidelity, and pornography miles ahead of "'til death do us part." At the risk of losing close friends and his side of the family, she initiates the divorce. Two beautiful children are stuck in the middle. No money and an abrupt career change. There are a lot of tears in her lemon drop martini. She survives, of course. Then, she soars. She is committed to helping others navigate their own rocky ice-capped mountains.

While friends are perfecting their lemon meringue pies and sharing those mouth-watering photos on Facebook, this 49-year-old is letting her "new" husband grocery shop and prepare meals for our family. She would rather be helping clients to become soulfully self-reliant and teach them to stand in respect to their own evolution. Our family is complete with two young adults and a 7-year-old. Life continues with its unexpected curveballs and challenges. They often cause some emotional upheaval. She's got the tools and gray hair to gracefully find her way through the other side of each of these lessons.

The mature lemon tree in our backyard bears the most fragrant fruit each year. We have so much. We enjoy what we can and then load the rest into an old red Radio Flyer wagon. We leave it by the community mailbox with a "Help Yourself" sign. Within a day or two, the wagon is empty, and it gets wheeled back home to await next year's harvest.

I'm not sure what our neighbors use their lemons for, and it doesn't really matter to me. I simply enjoy knowing that we've been able to pass them on for good use. Life is like that, you know?

We live inside our own experiences and make what we can out of them. The key is to take a look inside our stories and find the gift that is born out of our trials and tragedies.

The basic lemon itself is a thing of beauty and possibility, just like we are.

Why this book? Why these stories?

This anthology demonstrates how we, as human beings, can overcome obstacles through personal growth and soulful discovery. The incredible women featured in this book selflessly share their stories with relentless gratitude and a vision more powerful than their fear.

As you indulge in these narratives, you'll see that life's lemons become catalysts for businesses, nonprofits, products, services, organizations, and movements. We share a collective desire to turn tragedy into triumph, to heal wounds, to stop generational abuse patterns, and to leave the world a better place than it was when we got here.

It is an invitation for you to do the same.

I'm honored and humbled to have been asked by Michelle Faust to write this Foreword. I've known Michelle for a few years and am in awe of her strength, perseverance, and zest for learning and life. Michelle has enough of her own "lemons to lemonade" experiences to fill these pages and to provide us with guidance and inspiration. But, like the mature lemon tree in my backyard, Michelle knows when we open ourselves up and include others, it's a much sweeter experience.

As Michelle has invited women to participate in the creation of this book, a mindful community has formed. Each contributor has shown up in her greatness. Each of us has offered our unique gifts and talents to this growing community. And each of us has candidly shared how we are currently stepping out of our comfort zone and growing ... again. Myself included.

We are all in this together, and we invite you to be part of this collective.

It is my hope that you'll cuddle up with this book and melt into these pages as you read them. Let these women pour into your heart and mind. Let their courage, strength, and resolve spark something within you.

Your story matters. Don't leave your lemons on the tree.

With love, light, and leadership,
Karen

# Introduction

My first podcasting experience was a show called Rhino Nation. It was an offshoot of my content writing business. I interviewed all kinds of successful entrepreneurs and business leaders. While podcasting wasn't paying my bills, it opened the door to powerful people and incredible connections. Business leaders wanted to talk to me and share their stories. I had always been on the asking end, not the receiving end.

As both a content writer and podcast host, I saw my community grow into a circle of inspiring, amazing, and courageous women. While I found the men I interviewed had some of these characteristics too, a common theme emerged with the women. Their vision was far stronger than their fears. Success came to them from strength and determination. The women were more open to talking about their struggles and accepting support than men. More importantly, they were more likely to take a negative experience and change the way they saw themselves and the world. I was so fascinated by their stories and felt privileged to be able to share them with the world. Meanwhile, they gained the exposure they deserved and earned.

As I heard so many of these successes over struggle-type stories, I began to envision a book sharing what it took for these women to survive and then thrive. The Lemonade Stand was born. Not only are these stories powerful, but they are also helpful to women who are struggling in some aspect of their life.

As these women share their stories, you'll discover you are just as capable as any of these women in achieving more. The authors in this book do not have superpowers; they are just strong and determined women who set their sights on a goal and found a way to achieve it.

They've taught me a powerful lesson—while we are all just ordinary people, we can do extraordinary things if we choose.

As the idea of The Lemonade Stand started to gel and take form, even more amazing women not featured on the podcast started to come into my life. These women were excited to share their stories to help support and lift up other women. We were becoming a tribe. The Lemonade Stand project was far greater than the sum of its parts. We weren't just collaborating on a book, we were creating a community of love, faith, support, and generosity. After I began to benefit so greatly from this community of women, I began to think bigger and asked, "What is the potential for positively changing other women's lives through this project?"

The goal of publishing this book became a passion. My co-collaborators are just as determined as me to take the pain of their past and use it as a teaching tool to help their female comrades rise above their challenges. In the pages of this book, we have shared our vulnerabilities, mistakes, and shame, along with deep insights and revelations. We are soul sisters on a journey.

One of our authors, Elena Porter, created a t-shirt with a heart filled with words. These words are from all the authors and they represent the truth of their story. Each word, or word phrase, and the "why" is included in the author's biography. Please take the time to read them. They stand powerfully on their own, but add incredible richness and depth to their stories.

It is my hope that readers of The Lemonade Stand will join us in our mission to help women all over the world find freedom from fear, constraints, negative relationships, and outdated opinions. Through this freedom, we find peace, love, acceptance, and success.

This is The Lemonade Stand. Consider it a metaphorical supercharged recipe for making lemonade out of lemons.

~ **Michelle Faust**

# Michelle Faust

**Founder of Lemonade Legend**
**Author, Blogger, Content Writer, and Podcaster**

*H*eart Word: Fearless Attitude / I used to think that my achievements and breakthrough moments came from being Fearless. But that is not true because fear lives in us all the time and in different forms. It's how we choose to deal with fear that helps shape our destiny and find peace with our lives.

I am no stranger to turning lemons into lemonade. I've done it countless times throughout my personal and professional careers. The breakthrough moment for me was when I earned a pink slip while working in a traditional corporate career in pharmaceuticals.

For 20 years, I earned the status of top sales performer. Yet, when that pink slip arrived, I was told I no longer fit the image of the company. Youth and inexperience won. It was time to get the juicer out and make some lemonade out of all of those lemons.

As I churned those lemons around, I surrounded myself with leaders in the entrepreneurial world. By doing so, I rediscovered and embraced my lifelong passion for writing. At Lemonade Legend, I connect businesses to their specific target market by helping them optimize their message, brand, and written content.

I love to connect people, whether through the power and beauty of the written word or through a stimulating guest experience on my podcast, *Lemonade Legend*. My books, social posts, blogs, and *Lemonade Legend* podcast all celebrate the voice of entrepreneurs and small business owners who have tackled lemons and created amazing versions of lemonade opportunities.

# The Big Squeeze: Creating the Lemonade Stand

## By Michelle Faust

I'm 37 years old, divorced, a single parent, and down on my luck. I am barely scraping by as a Boutique Foods broker. My child support is zero as my ex is unemployed again. Life was throwing at me more lemons than usual, and I knew it was time to make some lemonade. I realized I was the only one who could change my destiny, and I was ready to do some squeezin'.

That was when serendipity intervened. I had an opportunity for a career change, and I didn't want to screw it up. A friend referred me to a hiring manager for a pharmaceutical position. I got the interview. When I walked in, her body language let me know I was clearly wasting her time. Her cruel condescending nature left me totally intimidated. When I stammered or messed up on a question, she rolled her eyes. Needless to say, I not only didn't get the job, it was extremely humiliating. But, I gave it my best as I walked away with my tail tucked behind my legs.

Much to my surprise, several weeks later, I received a call back as the contract sales force was expanding. When the hiring manager asked, "Would you like to come in for another interview?" I said to myself, "Wow, I either did something that impressed her, or she is hard up for candidates!" Whatever the case, I was thankful for another opportunity. This time she hired me. Praise be to God, for the first time in my life, I felt like I might have a chance of a real career.

During the paperwork process, she asked me to send copies of several items, including my university degree. There was dead silence. She had never asked me if I had a degree. I didn't lie because I didn't have to, she assumed I had a degree. At that moment, she realized her error. She just wanted to be done with this assignment, so she said she would bury it and get me on board. She made it clear that this was a temporary contract, so without a degree, I would be at a disadvantage to be hired for additional contracts. I enrolled at The University of Phoenix right away. Fortunately, I had about half of a degree's worth of credits. For two years, I worked my fanny off, studied and achieved a 3.83 GPA, and raised my two girls alone.

Not only was I enrolled in school, but I was also entering into a brand-new industry which required intense medical training and time demands. My girls were 10 and 6 at the time, and their dad was living in another state. This career change and attending college meant sacrificing time with my family, friends, and outside interests. My girls suffered because I couldn't spend the kind of "after work" time with them as they needed. Mothers feel guilty enough as it is having to work and raise children. I barely participated in parenting for those two years of getting my degree. But somehow we survived. At this point, my father was in a nursing home dying of liver failure, and my mother didn't understand what an accomplishment my career was. She probably would have preferred that I stayed home with my girls.

I made more money than I ever made in pharmaceutical sales. It required a level of professionalism I had never experienced before. It was intoxicating. I knew I had been given a gift when I first got hired, and I was dedicated to not lose out on this opportunity. This is where I learned to work hard and put my life skills to work. I told the little self-doubt girl on my shoulder who didn't think I would ever be in a high paying job to go away. It was tremendously exciting and ruthless at the same time. Pharma is a very competitive, high-earning, dog-eat-dog world. I was surrounded by young, sharp-looking, intellectually-quick coworkers.

I struggled to keep up, but I continued to work harder. Everyone else could rely on their personalities and fitting in. I had to rely on results, winning awards, and knocking it out of the park. I did that from year one.

Pharmaceuticals is a cutthroat business involving a lot of greed and competition. It is also very youth-oriented. To fit in, you need to dress like all that big money you are making. Because I was entering the game at age 37, all my money went to my kids and my savings. I couldn't justify spending $200–$300 on a purse or a pair of shoes. So, not only did I not look the part, I didn't behave the part. I'm smart, but not quick-witted and I don't blend well in groups.

The contract was unexpectedly pulled early but Novartis, the hiring company of the contract force, was growing internally. The hiring manager hired me almost on the spot as we had worked together previously. I continued to be a strong member of the team, earning respect more for performance than the easy, happy-go-lucky personalities of my colleagues. My extra efforts and work paid off. I won a long list of awards and achievements.

Eleven years in, I was tired of mass-market sales (selling to primary care providers). I started looking for a position in specialty sales which is the crème de la crème of pharma jobs. There was a position open in the Cystic Fibrosis division, and I wanted it. I hit it off well with the hiring manager, but during our talks, a hiring freeze took effect. I continued to look and interview for other specialty positions, but I never took my eye off that prize. I continued to call the manager regularly throughout the freeze until he finally said, "Michelle, I promise to hire you the moment I can!" True to his word, he hired me. It was a much smaller division than mass-market, and I had much more autonomy. It was a great step up in my career.

Pharmaceuticals was a tough industry for me. For 19 years, I sucked it up because I wanted to prove to both myself and the world that I not only mattered, but that I also contributed. I wanted to demonstrate that I could be successful in this grueling environment. It shaped everything about me professionally and personally. I accomplished a long list of sales awards which really spoke for what I was capable of. I had stayed away from specialty for a long time because I was afraid to step out of my comfort zone. But I did it, and it was truly a feeling of stepping out of the fearful attitude and creating a vision that said, "I've got this."

Being successful in the field of pharmaceutical sales was especially incredible for me. You see, I was born with a significant high-frequency hearing loss. (High-frequency sounds are soft and high-pitched sounds like soft consonants, whistles, bird chirps, etc.) At a certain frequency, I am profoundly deaf. Throughout my childhood, I learned how to compensate for this disability. These are the skills that I relied on and honed to perfection that enabled me to work in the demanding field of pharma.

Problems for me didn't really start until elementary school. I was regularly called out of class for "special education" speech lessons. I couldn't hear soft sounds like S, F, TH, and so on. This was the first memory of being singled out and different. Every time I heard my name called over the school intercom to go to speech lessons, I could feel the eyes of my classmates on me, the heavy label on my forehead that said, "I am DIFFERENT." My speech teacher made me repeat, "Sally sells seashells by the seashore," until I wanted to vomit. I hated that speech teacher! She made me determined to learn on my own.

I was different, but I didn't truly appreciate in what way. I couldn't compare myself to the hearing world because I didn't know how great the difference was. I remember sometimes thinking that it would be better to be completely deaf because then people would understand what my disability was. Mine was a "silent" or hidden challenge because I appeared and acted normal. I felt some shame and tried to hide it as best I could. It embarrassed me, so I spent my life as a fraud, trying to be someone I wasn't.

I didn't make friends easily, but I was fortunate that my classmates were either compassionate or ignored me. I never experienced true bullying. Teasing, yes, and getting the sense that people perceived me as stupid, yes, but no bullying.

When I was 9, my oldest sister contracted spinal meningitis, which resulted in about a two-year struggle she eventually lost. She was flown to the National Institutes of Health in Bethesda, Maryland, where my mother stayed by her side for over a year. During this time, my grandmothers raised me. My father turned to alcohol which only got worse throughout his life. My sister's death impacted my mom's mental health in a big way. Since neither of my parents were there to lift me up emotionally through my challenges, I had to develop a sense of independence. I felt a bit like a lost child. Throughout my childhood I became my own best friend and advocate. I was my own mentor, teacher, and spiritual guide. I learned to depend on myself to learn, grow, and achieve.

Reading was the best way for me to experience the world. I believe it set me up for being a good student during my later years. Being around people who laughed and were engaged with TV, movies, plays, and musical lyrics was frustrating for me. My all-time favorite book is Gone with the Wind, all 862 pages of it. I must have read it a dozen times. There was a part of me that embraced my quiet world. It provided me with a certain level of comfort.

I tried my first hearing aid around the age of 21. I think it took me that long because of the chaos and dysfunctional behaviors in my childhood. I periodically have tried new technology through-out my adulthood. The two main problems I have had with aids are that my high-frequency loss is so profound while my lower frequencies are near normal. That is much more difficult to cor-rect than an across-the-board loss. They would have to power it up for the high sounds which would blow me out of my chair. The biggest problem is that my brain has never been exposed to true natural sounds. When a baby is born, their brains are assaulted with loud, obnoxious noises (probably why they cry) to which their brains eventually filter out and adapt. My brain has never gone through that process, so wearing hearing aids was a painful and completely distracting experience. I preferred to retreat into my safe, quiet world.

It is a bit of a mystery to me. But I simply refused to behave, or believe that I was any different. It's almost like I worked more at fooling myself than I did other people. I just lived and worked within the normal world. But at the same time, I look back and remember being alone often. When I went to church youth camp for several summers, I remember being a bit of a loner. When we had downtime, I would usually go read or take solitude in the woods instead of hanging out with the other kids. The space of silence and solitude has always comforted me.

Despite a lack of self-assurance, tons of self-doubt, and con-tinuous frustrations, deep down, I believed I was smart and exceptional. I learned to adapt and compensate. I read lips, I stud-ied body language, and I sought the help of trusted friends to help in correcting my speech. When I interviewed for a job, I would study hard to learn the industry. When I got a job, I worked harder than the rest to be at least as good. The jobs I went after were all sales-related, which is difficult for a hearing-impaired person. I remember one doctor of audiology (ENT) couldn't compre-hend how I managed in sales. But strangely enough, I liked the communication and meeting one-on-one with people. My skill set for developing relationships was very good. Looking back, it is probably because unlike other people, I can't afford to look away when talking to someone. By reading their body language, I knew when to shift gears in the conversation.

Besides the hearing loss, I also had a condition called hyperhidrosis which is excessive sweating of the feet and hands. If I went to shake someone's hand, I would leave their hand literally dripping in sweat. Another sour lemon as it contributed significantly to my self-doubt. I later had surgery to correct this.

Prior to my pharmaceutical career, I plugged along most of my adult life working in a variety of sales, mostly in entrepreneurial situations. I brokered boutique food and unique baskets to gift shops and gift basket makers. For years I sold and installed both real and fake plants for offices and homes. It was never quite enough to take care of my two girls. I received absolutely no financial contribution from my ex-husband. He continued to live in Chicago for seven years, so the girls went to visit him during summer break and at Christmas. This allowed me to concentrate on my career, but being without my girls at Christmas was hard. One Christmas I painted my bedroom.

In 2011, a new cystic fibrosis drug was getting ready to hit the market. This highly specialized biotech drug would change the face of how the disease was treated. One of the managers on my team was hired into this new company, and she was recruiting many people from within the Novartis CF division. I raised my hand and was given an interview.

It was unlike any interview I have ever had. The panel consisted of company heavyweights. They would ask typical questions like, "Tell me a time when…" But, the trick was they wanted me to create a storyline with a common theme. I had to subtitle each incident and then title the whole story. It was kind of like creating a storyboard where you showed a graphic representation of how your video will be shot, play by play. It was their way of determining if you were a quick thinker and creative. The whole process made me wonder if I was bright enough for the position.

It proved to be the toughest interview I have ever had in my life. They wanted, and knew they could get, the absolute top people in the country. Getting this position was my triumphant moment. I was finally in my element. I had a great territory, covering Southern California, selling a highly specialized biotech drug. I developed great relationships with my clinics, and the world was my oyster.

I had reached the pinnacle of my career when I was hired into biotech. It was still hard work and a challenge with my hearing loss, but I was rocking it with my numbers and my business relationships. I figured about five years in this position, I could retire as all my hard work would be rewarded by then. That was not to be. My time was up. This group of coworkers were of a different breed. Even though I continued to have an excellent track record, I recognized I didn't fit in here. It was a small company where everyone knew everyone. I suspected high-level management felt I wasn't as smart, savvy, or hip as the rest of the crew. Three years into the job, a new manager came on board and was ready to make some changes. Three of us (myself included) out of a seven-member division lost our jobs. It just so happened we were the three oldest members of the team. Coincidence? Hmmm.

It was a brutal experience; I have never been treated with such disrespect and callous intent. I was completely devastated. I didn't think I would survive it. I cannot give justice through the written word to the level of emotional pain I felt. People lose their jobs every day. Shit happens, but this was a calculated move to oust me from a position that I had worked hard for and deserved to have. The biggest blow was it was all because someone with a higher pay grade didn't like me. There was never any consideration for how hard I worked, or how loyal and honest I was. After 56 years of fighting hard to be more than my disability, I felt like I had finally lost the battle. But, I persevered.

I went through interviews surrounded by 20-something-year-old blondes in their Jimmy Choo shoes. I had interview after interview ad nauseam. I looked at other professions, such as financial services and even successfully completed my Series 65 License, an intense period of study to pass a punishing financial exam to be licensed as a Registered Financial Advisor. I did this at the urging and encouragement of a close friend who wanted me to work for his firm. But in the end, I had to be true to myself, my passion, and my desire to prove my worth beyond sales awards.

This was about the time where I learned (in hindsight) to stop trying to hide my hearing loss. After I was fired, I became more comfortable with sharing my disability. If people couldn't accept me that way, especially after so many accomplishments, then I didn't want to be around them. I also learned to appreciate the power of money and achievement. I had made a lot of money and lived conservatively, and I had a list of achievements that spoke for themselves. I didn't need to feel afraid or powerless.

So, I picked myself up out of depression and self-loathing, and I dusted myself off. I needed to move forward. All those lemons were ripe for making lemonade. It was time to reinvent myself. By combining my love of writing, my skills to easily learn new things, and my ability to develop solid relationships, I launched my own business as a content writer. Sometimes I really miss my paycheck and benefits. But I am so liberated from being with people who have the power to control my life and feelings of self-worth.

I'll take my sour lemons along with my successes. I've learned more about myself, about business, and relationships in the last three years than I did in 19 years of pharma. In the process, I discovered it was okay to be me, and it was okay to fail. I could dream big and jump into the world of successful entrepreneurs and be accepted. I had spent too much time listening to and being influenced by well-meaning friends and family. Their advice was always to go on the path of least resistance. They encouraged me to get another sales job, collect a paycheck for a few more years, and then retire. I finally found peace when I decided to go after my dream. I may not ever make the kind of money I previously did, or I might. Either way, it's okay, because for the first time in my life, I'm living it as the real me.

I am not defined by my physical realities; I am defined by my soul and inner desires. I am a child of God, who loves me no matter what. Through the gift of faith, I've not only survived, but I have thrived. Who I am is more than the sum of my parts. I will leave a legacy that my children will be proud of and learn from. So, they too can be the best version of themselves. I encourage you to chase your dreams. You'll most likely encounter lemons in the process, but you can always make lemonade.

# Donita Bath Wheeler

**Cancer, Life, and Survivor Coach/ Podcaster**

*H*eart Word: No Fear / I've operated from a place of fear for 30+ years, and finally after watching my mother-in-law take her last breath, I decided to stand up and face my fear. I had to stop hiding behind helping and face my very own fear by myself!

Donita "Mama Bear" Wheeler is a survivor of many cancers including triple-negative breast cancer. During that brave battle, she beat the odds of a 1% survival rate. Her experiences living through, between, and after her cancer diagnosis has made Donita an incredible voice on survivorship, facing fear, and the many topics that cancer families face.

A former first-grade teacher, Donita has a thirst for knowledge that drives her to understand all facets of survivorship, prevention, and the concept of facing fear. She shares her knowledge during a weekly podcast and through her social followers. The Mama Bear name suits Donita as she is protective of her "cubs," all who are inspired by her story.

The original Mama Bear nickname comes from her deep love for her husband, Whitney, and her two grown sons. Donita enjoys speaking on the subject of survivorship and cancer coaching overall to large audiences globally.

# I Am the One Percent ... You Can't Kill Me

## By Donita Wheeler

Why would I want to claim to be one percent of anything? There is a zero percent chance that you will get through life with zero percent fear. We all have an innately human response of primal fear that we can't do anything about. Because of what has happened in my life, I've been able to face my fears and grow as a result. Here's my story.

I am standing on the beach, looking at the clear Caribbean waters that surround Hollywood, Florida. It's those greens and turquoise blues that calm and empower me. This place relaxes my body. I'm able to naturally breathe and smile as I gaze upon the water.

Today is different from most days. Today, I received the news I had cancer—not just regular cancer, but triple-negative breast cancer (TNBC), with a survivor rate of one percent. TNBC is a more aggressive cancer and has a poorer prognosis than other types of breast cancer. Besides that, there's a higher chance of reoccurrence and/or metastasizing quickly.

Triple-negative breast cancer tests negative for estrogen receptors, progesterone receptors, and excess HER2 protein. This means the cancer's growth is not fueled by the hormone's estrogen and progesterone, or by the HER2 protein. Because of this, triple-negative breast cancer does not respond to hormonal therapy medicines or medicines that target HER2 protein receptors.

As I stood upon my sacred spot overlooking the water, I thought, "How dare cancer intrude on me here." Quickly, the happiness associated with this place went to uncharted fear. I was instantly thrown into the cancer vortex where the light and love of my favorite spot turned dark, black, and stormy. Like quicksand, my world was ripped out from under me. All I knew and understood was gone when I heard the words, "Your biopsy came back positive for cancer." Just. Like. That.

As the call came on a Friday, it gave me the weekend to really sit with, "You have cancer." Those words kept going through my mind. That weekend I didn't know anything about my diagnosis. I was in shock. When we received the diagnosis on Friday, I didn't want to disrupt the family vacation, so my husband and I kept the news to ourselves until we returned from our trip. To this day, my two boys say very little about my cancer.

Things happened so quickly once I got an appointment with the oncologist. But there was a waiting list. Sit with that for a minute. I had been diagnosed with cancer with a one percent survival rate, and now I was on a waiting list. However, sometimes my one percent works in my favor.

My son and I were headed to the dentist. Before I picked him up, I stopped at the oncologist's office and picked up the paperwork I needed to complete. My dentist happened to see my paperwork and asked, "Do you need to get in to see her?" Her was my oncologist. I said, "Yes, I was diagnosed with breast cancer right before we went on vacation. Without skipping a beat, he said, "I can help you. Give me your cell number."

It turns out the oncologist was a patient of his. As a result, I got a phone call the next morning for an appointment for the following day at 1:00 pm. I figured there was about a one percent chance of my dentist getting me into my oncologist in one day. She ordered another ultrasound and a PET scan. During this time, I refused to look up any information on the Internet about TNBC. Denial worked to keep my worrying at bay. In fact, I did the perfect ostrich performance for a year and a half.

Then, I had six biopsies on my right breast and one on the left breast, and they were all negative. I did have a few more biopsies after my treatment was over, and I was terrified each time, but it became less and less as I was beginning to finally master the entire diagnosis. I had a lumpectomy in the right breast, and then I had the four rounds of TAC, a medication used to treat breast cancer, and 28 rounds of radiation.

I vividly recall my first chemo treatment. They put my port in a few weeks earlier, and they tested and tested it. They run this saline solution through it, and you can taste and smell it. That smell to this day makes me gag. On this day, I was all ready to go. I arrived at the oncology office and went back into the chemo ward and sat in my chair with my goody bag. Society has chemo goody bags covered, and I was prepared. I was not prepared for my port not working. They had to use my veins after about an hour of flushing it with that saline, and it still was not working. Somebody mumbled about it being odd that it didn't work. I wanted to laugh and say, "You haven't met me and my odds yet!" I was hurting badly.

The night before I went in for chemo, I was on some super strong steroids. I was cleaning the house at 3:00 am. Seriously, scrubbing the floors. It was a good thing as it would be another two years before I could do anything like that again! The steroids actually had me excited for chemo, although I was super amped up and super NOT patient. We were there for 12 hours that day. I barely made it home before I laid down in my bed. I was physically unable to move for the rest of the evening and most of the next day. I wanted and tried to move, but my body was like, "Lady, you are not moving after that onslaught of chemicals no matter how hard you try and make me move." And that's exactly what happened.

I could not make it to my bathroom, which was three feet from my bed. I kept telling myself to get up but my body would not move. It was almost indescribable. My body was absolutely not playing. I did nothing other than lie there feeling horrible. I thought a few hours went by, but I think it was more like a week until I finally got out of bed after that first chemo treatment.

My treatments were spaced four weeks apart for recovery. I love that—like you can recover from chemo in four weeks only to be dosed again. My husband, Whitney, had a very stressful demanding job, and my two boys, William and Nick, were in eighth and tenth grade. My husband did everything for me that week, or more accurately, for at least six months. He got up every morning and got the boys off to school, and then headed to work. He made sure I was able to help myself while he was gone. In order to keep up with his workload, he would often work until 2:00, 3:00, or 4:00 am.

I hated being incapacitated, but I hated the thought of being dead even more. So, I didn't fight it. The only fight I could actually handle was my fight against cancer. Day by day, my self-esteem, self-worth, body, and mind were slowly disintegrating into such a dark, lonely, sad, and desperate place. I didn't recognize who I saw in the mirror. I was huge—I looked like a Macy's Day Parade float of myself.

One of the things I was actually excited about (try not to judge me here) was losing weight. I have always been, let's be generous and say chubby. I was truly excited to be thin. I mean I didn't know anyone with cancer who was chubby. My dad lost 60 pounds with his cancer. It didn't happen for me—I gained 60 pounds. This just made it so much worse. My silver lining was more of a buttery lining. As a result, I was becoming withdrawn, ghastly white, beaten down, unsure of myself, and so very scared of everything.

The fear of dying and being disfigured was constantly on my mind. I found myself doing mindless activities that just wasted time. I watched so many movies; I couldn't think while watching a movie. I slept a lot because I was so tired from the chemo and radiation, but my mind was wandering. I was suddenly scared of laundry detergent, conventional food, shampoos, acrylic nails, alcohol, germs, dairy, meat, and wheat (which I actually turned out to be allergic to). I was constantly weighing the good and the bad regarding chemicals I used in my home and what I put in or on my body. This literally made me crazy. I doubted everything I had ever known, and all from lifelessly lying in my bed or on the couch, a full year after my last radiation. My hair was growing back, my scars were beginning to heal, and my body was adjusting to the new normal. But my mind held steadfastly to the fear growing bigger and bigger inside of me.

When I reached the survivor state, I kept hearing, "You're done now, you can go back to your life!" There has never been such a false statement. As a cancer survivor, the real work, walking the cancer path, only actually begins with the onset of survivorship. Positive comments from people meant to cheer me up did exactly the opposite. I was feeling lost and alone. But then one day, I woke up and decided I was going to begin fighting the fear. I was going to leave the house and talk to people and live my life again. I got the strength and courage from my favorite one percent statistic—I was going to use it to fight and WIN!

I started keeping a journal of my thoughts, and I forced myself to write a positive word each day, several times a day. Once I got the hang of it, I started listing goals like getting a manicure, getting my hair trimmed, and leaving the house. These were things I loved to do prior to the diagnosis and wanted to do after the diagnosis. I was slowly beginning to feel like myself again. I was also going to beginner's yoga, where I learned to meditate and breathe. This was a good thing as my cancer journey was far from over.

Later, I was twice-diagnosed with ovarian cancer. I had a partial hysterectomy when the first ovarian tumor turned cancerous. A few short years later, another tumor became cancerous, and they removed each and every lady part I had left! The second hysterectomy mentally destroyed me.

It was nine days after the full hysterectomy that I got in my car and drove to the beach with a brick and a rope in my hand. I walked to the edge of the water and I just stood there. What felt like three days was probably about ten minutes. I don't recall thinking about anything or even realizing I was standing there. Something happened, maybe it was a seagull that snapped me out of whatever trance I was in.

I was suddenly standing at the edge of the water with the brick in my hand. It felt like an out-of-body experience. Although I don't remember getting in the car, driving to the beach, walking down to the water to jump in with the brick, I know it happened. I know that my logic kicked in at some point because I was a really good swimmer, and there was no way I could have drowned with just a brick.

I am so grateful that my Higher Self did not let me die. When I came out of my trance, I was hungry. I went to my favorite sushi restaurant on the beach. I ordered rice noodle soup and a glass of tea. I ate a few bites of the soup and then took my tea to the car. As I sat there, I was digesting a whole lot more than food. For some reason, I did not die that day. It wasn't my time.

After dropping to this new low, I finally gathered the strength to face my fears and grow to the best of my being. I decided I needed to be true to myself and who I was. I hired a therapist to help me, too. The new survivor in me seemed to have more guts than the person I was before having cancer.

It has taken me ten years to reach this state of mind, the state of feeling good about myself and strong enough to be able to withstand the even more challenging events that would eventually take place. Through my strength, I gained clarity. I quit a job that was not serving me. I broke up with some lifelong friends who were not good for me. I started to question relationships that I felt made my spidey senses go crazy. As I started to listen to myself, the strangest pattern began to emerge. The people I was letting go of were being replaced with people who were feeding my soul. It was through these relationships that I found the catalyst that changed my constant questioning. I was learning to accept and love the new post-cancerous me.

Fear is an ever-evolving beast that will torment us for the rest of our lives unless we resolve it. I am not talking about the healthy fear that keeps us out of danger; that is a good healthy fear that doesn't need conquering. I'm talking about the unresolved fear, the buried deep fear, the fear that escapes boundaries, and finally, the fear that makes or breaks you.

Fear stopped me in my tracks when I was in a bad car accident during college. Before the wreck, fear wasn't something I spent a lot of time thinking about. Sure, there were the normal fears that kids face when growing up, like moving and starting over with friends or going to the principal's office. But, this fear was different. I could no longer be ignorant when it came to fear. Fear became real and powerful.

The car wreck altered everything and impacted how I approach driving, even today. I had been out drinking with friends the night the accident happened. Back in the 1980s, during college, that's what we did—we went to bars and drank and danced. This particular night, the bar was closing, and it was time to go home. I had stopped drinking about halfway through the night when I realized my friend wasn't stopping. We got into his car, and I began driving. As I lived in the city next to him, I was a little lost. When I missed a turn, he suddenly pulled up the emergency brake. The car spun around. He said he could drive us home because he lived just around the corner. We switched seats, and I became the passenger. It had rained that night, and as we approached an intersection, a police officer clocked us at 85 mph on his radar gun. As we hit the water and were hydroplaning, by the grace of God (or maybe my one percent tag), I reached over and put on my seat belt. At that moment, we hit a telephone pole going 85 mph. There is no logical reason I should have lived that night, but I did.

That wreck turned out to be the catalyst that I didn't fully understand for decades. Fear began controlling my life. Once you become intimate with fear, there is little going back. The fear of my car wreck didn't come close to the fear I felt when I was diagnosed with triple-negative breast cancer and given a one percent chance of living. I didn't deal with the fear then; I didn't deal with the fear of watching my mother-in-law slowly die from cancer. I didn't even deal with the fear when my dad passed away or when my husband lost his job. Something was holding me back.

I was losing relationships, I was losing my life as I knew it, my husband didn't have a job, and we had spent 24/7 together for over a year and were not doing well with each other's company. For eight months, we took care of his terminally ill mother in a strange place, living in someone else's house, away from all we knew, and all of our support. After she died, when we moved home to our empty house, things began to fall apart. Somewhere in between crying and screaming and giving up, I realized we both were burying our fear of all things that had happened to us.

It was through a day of tears that I was able to finally process what had been boiling underneath the surface for years. It was truly a pivotal and defining moment for me, as I was able to pinpoint the fear that was MY starting point for facing and controlling it.

Yes, it was the wreck that I had in college when I was 20. As I was pinpointing my original fear catalyst, I was establishing a baseline for my pinpointed fear. That meant each time I feared something big or little in my life, it sent me back to that car wreck. It was from this baseline that I was able to track down the growing fear and begin the healing process.

In the middle of all this fear and confusion, I had a huge idea inside of me that I knew I wouldn't be able to do unless I faced the fear. Six years after my TNBC diagnosis, I became a Mama Bear Cancer Coach. I named my company Mama Bear because I truly feel it is my calling to metaphorically wrap my arms around anyone who is experiencing cancer and be the strong force they need in their corner.

Early on, I worked with clients to help them decipher what is commonly known as the cancer maze. I view diagnosis, treatment, and survivorship as the three stages on the cancer path. I worked with clients through all of these stages.

Something was still lacking in my business, and I wasn't sure what that was. I reached a true turning point while caregiving during my mother-in-law's final stages of cancer. The experience of watching my mother-in-law take her last breath allowed me to take away the fear of someone dying right in front of me.

Even after experiencing the incredible amount of fear associated with hearing statements like, "you have cancer," "your nephew has leukemia," "your Dad has cancer," and "your mother-in-law is terminally ill," it was through those experiences that I gained my strength and found my calling as Donita Mama Bear.

While writing this story, I didn't let the fear of sharing it stop me. I used my fear process. Because of this, I am digging deeper to offer myself as a beacon in the survivorship world. I am passionate about sharing my experiences, my personal story, and modeling to others how to navigate fear. We all need a survivor safe place. I'm not a superhero, but I have found a way to break through the fear barrier. I AM determined to make sure every survivor has the ability to process their fear, and use it as their very own superpower.

What do I have to say to cancer? I am the one percent; you can't kill me!

## Aislinn Ellis

**Professional Organizer/ Owner and Founder of AskAisi**

*H*eart Word: Purge / I've consumed so much hate and other people's trauma, drama, and junk, which only added to my own. I'm purging all of that and moving forward. Seeing the light, the heart and the soul of the good in this world and reminding others that it's there if they seek it …This is where my journey leads.

Aislinn N. Ellis, AKA Ms. Organized, is on a mission to reach and motivate 25,000,000 people with her motto "Why Organize? ... Because it matters!" She is the owner and operator of Ask Aisi, LLC, and is constantly developing her company, Always Organized – Workspace Solutions. Best known for her personable nature, she is dedicated to public speaking, mentoring, and connecting others. She's a brutally honest woman of faith and community.

Early on, she knew there were great things in store for her, and she dared to dream of running an empire. She became President of the Future Business Leaders of America in her high school and went on to win the State FBLA Public Speaking Competition. As a survivor of domestic violence, she knows all too well how precious and fleeting life can be. In 2017, she quit the family business and followed her father's entrepreneurial spirit. She worked hard and became a professional organizer – her true calling. This passion is endorsed by her mother, who confirms that as a child, Aislinn would re-organize her room every week.

She believes it made her feel she could create order within her chaotic world. A middle child with a brother on either side, she did not have the easiest time growing up. Forced to leave her family home at 17, she has had to meet, greet, and beat all sorts of obstacles. She sees chaos in people's lives and wants nothing more than to teach and motivate them to control it in ways that work for them. Arizona has been her home for nearly 30 years, and she's going to make sure it's organized ... because it matters!

# PRESS FORWARD ...
## It'll Get Easier

### By Aislinn Ellis

People tell me that I'm strong. I'm resilient. I'm a survivor. I have lived 100 lives in my short 38 years. Most of the time, I don't feel that way. I feel flawed and so broken, but I'm still giving myself time to heal. Telling this story is part of my healing.

My given name, Aislinn (Irish), is inspired by a romance novel my mother read while she was pregnant with me, The Wolf and the Dove by Kathleen Woodiwiss. Aislinn means "dream," which describes me perfectly. I remember my kindergarten class reading Alison in Wonderland as I daydreamed—staring out the window. The other kids teased me, saying I was like Alison in the book. I cried. When I told my parents, my dad's response was to call me by a different name: Nikki (short for Nichole, my middle name), which I adopted for half of my life. Not a perfect solution for bullying, but he tried.

As you may imagine, the name change didn't stop the bullying, or the fact that I've always been a dreamer ... a romantic. I trust people unless they give me a reason not to. Sometimes it's too late and they're already too close.

My dad always had an extreme way of dealing with trouble. He grew up on the streets of Mississippi, finally leaving home when his mom shot at him for being "stubborn." I don't know much about his life before my mom, but I do have 16 older half siblings from different women. My parents met in Chicago while my mother was in the US Air Force. They were polar opposites in every way—different races (Caucasian and African American), different values, and different goals. There's a 16-year age gap between them. My dad was a charmer—the mechanic who fixed my mom's car, and she was in way over her head. Once they were married, the Air Force wouldn't allow her to divorce him. When issues with my dad came up, we got transferred. I've lived in Texas, Colorado, Maine, New Hampshire, and, finally, Arizona.

## Schools hated my dad, too.

In Maine, when some kids called my siblings and I "Ni*ger Babies," my father brought his shotgun to school and threatened the principal.

Of course, it wasn't all bad. By my bed are pictures of my mom holding me at Christmas, and my younger brother Kyle playing on the floor next to us and, in a separate picture, me sitting on my dad's knee. We never lacked anything, and that was thanks to my mom and all of her hard work.

He was a true-blood entrepreneur, but kept most of the money he made for himself, leaving my mom working two or three jobs to provide for our family. I remember them yelling. My mother begging for money for food and bills and my father insisting she had to pay him back when she got paid. He paid our babysitters with drugs or strip jewelry or any other trade. I know he did his best, but I learned quickly what to expect from men.

When I was three, I vividly remember hearing them scream down the hall – my father presenting a choice to my mother: he would either get sex or he would beat her. In my young brain, a truth was solidified, "sex is power." I found that out for myself too soon.

Despite everything, every kid wants to be with their dad. I was no exception. I loved riding in his beat-up truck to his auto shop on 75th and Glendale in Phoenix, easily a 45-minute drive from our home in Buckeye. He called me "Nick Knack." I hung out in the waiting room and played Pac-Man while he worked. I would talk and laugh with 24-year-old Johnny who somehow managed the arcades, happy to have a friend.

Only, he wasn't my friend. One day, Johnny pushed me into the auto shop's filthy bathroom and pushed inside me. I was 9. My dad was 100 feet away, but I didn't scream. I didn't like it but I didn't know what rape was. This fit my standard for men. I want to call myself naïve, but how could I have known at 9 years old? That's when men swoop in, when you're fragile and pretty.

The next day when I bled, my mom thought I had started my period. My white dress was all laid out for the birthday party that afternoon. She gave me a pad. We never discussed it, and I'm still not sure if she knew, but she never let me go back to my dad's auto shop. She said it was no place for a young lady.

After that, life fell into a steady pace. I kissed a lot of boys and did really well at school. My older brother Teil joined the military. My father's entrepreneurial spirit rubbed off on me, and I asked my mom if she would buy bulk bags of Jolly Ranchers at the Commissary and then let me sell them as individuals for 25 cents apiece at my school. I also worked a merchandising job on my mom's base from the time I was12 until I hit my sophomore year. At a Boyz II Men concert, I met my first real boyfriend, Derek. He was from Tempe and I was from Buckeye, so we'd meet up halfway between our houses at 75th Avenue or talk on the phone.

People who know me know I love to be involved in everything, and high school was no exception. I was on the auxiliary dance team and the flag team (the only freshman). I was also great at tennis. Until 9th grade, I played clarinet in band. One day I couldn't find my clarinet, and I looked everywhere. My mom had just finished making payments on it, so I never told anyone it was missing and I felt so guilty. I eventually learned after my dad died in 2004 that he dropped my clarinet off at the pawn shop for $50 and never went back for it.

My younger brother Kyle and I drove together to school every day. He actually taught me to drive. My sophomore year, Kyle came home with a truck. No one said anything, but everyone wondered where he got it—he was only 14. A few days later the police picked Kyle up at the Tasty Freeze for armed robbery. The truck belonged to his friend's grandfather. The trial went on for six months, and mom couldn't afford a lawyer, so Kyle was eventually sentenced to state prison for seven years. For what it's worth, I still don't think he did it. He was in detention the day it got jacked.

Regardless, the little stability my family did have was broken completely. My mom felt that she had let Kyle down. My dad detached.

Nobody asked me about me. Nobody cared.

I had tennis matches and band practice. No one came. I just showed up and did the best that I could. I wasn't eating, and there weren't clean clothes at home. My pervy math teacher bought my lunches.

Eventually, my school's Special Needs Administrator, Mrs. Palmer, asked me if everything was okay at home. I spilled everything. She suggested that we go talk to my parents: us and a psychologist. We sat in my family's living room and the psychologist told my dad, "Look, she's unhappy." My dad didn't skip a beat, retaliating, "Young girl, if you're unhappy there's the door. And you two weren't invited so get the f*ck out."

Mrs. Palmer let me stay at her house until senior year. She's probably the first heroine I can put a name to in my story. I know there were others; she's just the one I remember. The Palmers never hurt me and for the first time in my life I felt safe. They had dinner every night at 6:30 pm; we all talked about our day like I'd seen on TV. I tried not to be a bother. I cleaned, and I still worked the night shift with my mom until the early morning hours, slept for a few hours, and then went back to school.

Mrs. Palmer created a safe environment for me to challenge myself. I became the president of the Future Business Leaders of America at our school. I began to dream again. I wanted to run an empire. By then I already knew that I didn't want kids—I couldn't protect them, like I couldn't protect myself.

I qualified for the FBLA national public speaking competition, and the Palmers listened to me practice my speech over and over. My mom took me shopping for the perfect outfit. But when I won, no one was there. I floated through high school by myself.

While I was getting on with my life, my ex-boyfriend, Derek, got caught boosting cars and went to prison. I lost touch with him after that and started seeing other people.

My senior year, Marsha started asking me what I was planning after graduation. I had planned to stay with them for a while longer, but she strongly recommended I apply to college and get out on my own.

**College.**

My dad spent my college fund opening a doughnut shop in my name, Nikki's Donuts, which of course, failed. The Palmers helped me get into Yavapai Community College and bought me everything I needed. I wasn't honestly sure how I would get along with kids my age. By high school, I had one best friend, one cigarette, and one drink at a party. Sure enough, when school started my suitemates thought I was too "stuck up" because I wouldn't go out with them. The basketball team would hit on me—hassle me—until one night they decided to get the girl who was "too good for them." In my dorm, my roommates let them in while I was sleeping. I remember being so cold in that room. Night after night, one by one, they came in and raped me. I started having nightmares and I couldn't sleep. To this day, I can't sleep unless there are pillows surrounding me. Needless to say, I dropped out ... but I got my education. I wish I could say I reported them and got justice. But, that's not what happened. My framework told me it was my fault.

My older brother Teil was back from the Navy when I got home. I missed him so much. He was the only one I spent time with then—he made me feel like everything was going to be okay.

Valentine's Day before I turned 19, an employee at the Commissary relayed a gift from a secret admirer. I couldn't imagine who it was, but a girl on the Air Force base told me it was James, an older guy who worked at the commissary and at Circle K at the time. I was incredibly flattered. Turns out he had been watching me through my teenage life. We talked a few times, and he asked me out on our first date. This is a gentleman, I thought.

Before our date, we sat down on the bench and he immediately unzipped his pants. Looking back, I want to tell that girl to get up and walk away—I want to scream at her and grab her hand. But I can't. We went to Chili's for dinner, and that night I got pregnant.

We went out a few more times and then I got a call at work ... from his wife. I was floored. When I immediately broke it off with him, he promised me he would break up with her. For a while I thought he did. He would take me back to what I now know was a buddy's pad to "prove she had left." I found out later that his first marriage was a green card situation. He got her pregnant and shipped her back to Scotland.

We moved in together and I had my son, Aerick. For a while, everything was fine. James supported us financially and cared for Aerick. I was so happy. I read him the dictionary for the first year of his life. It was like treading water, though, and sometimes we slipped under financially. Soon after Aerick celebrated his first year, I went back to work to become the breadwinner, but it wasn't enough. One of our cars, for instance, was under threat of repossession. I worked hard and scraped together the payments, asking James to mail it in while I was at work. He didn't. They came for the car.

A few years later in August of 2004 my dad passed away from an aortic aneurysm. As he got older he battled heart conditions and diabetes. He softened over time. Regretting what he did to our lives, he apologized on more than one occasion. He was supportive. I remember when I got pregnant with Aerick he told me, "Baby girl, it's gonna be alright." He was a sweet grandpa, and it broke my heart to lose him so early.

Eventually James and I broke up, and I left—splitting time with my son. While I officially never lost custody of my son, my ex moved away against court orders. Without transportation, it was difficult going to see him. I thought about fighting it again in court but I just couldn't lose anymore. I hated his father for a long time for being so selfish and making it so hard for me to be with our son. It wasn't until later I found out he still wanted to be with me and was using our son to punish me because I didn't want to be with him.

My middle school boyfriend was due to get out of prison and so he contacted me again. He was brilliant with a degree from MIT, but he couldn't get a job because of his felony record. I was still in love with him, so we moved in together. He was a different person than I remembered. He had gotten himself addicted to meth, and for a while I thought being with me would help him remember who he was. I was wrong.

By the time I decided that I couldn't be with him anymore, he was already possessive–texting me constantly to find out where I was. If I didn't answer, all hell broke loose. One day, while I was at work, he sent me a video of him and my son on the sidewalk. He was smiling and had a sing-song tone, but his eyes were stone cold. He texted, "If you don't come home soon I'll push Aerick into the street." That was it. He had already put his hands on me more than once, but I couldn't bear the thought of my son hurt. I started making plans to escape.

The first time, I had everything ready. I got a new apartment, and I waited for Friday so I could take my son to his dad's. I took the day off work and I gathered my son's things. I begged his dad to keep him for a while. He said no and told me I had to figure it out. So, our normal exchange day came and I kissed my son good-bye with a wish and a prayer that it would all work out okay.

I spent one night in that apartment and walked down the steps in the morning to see Derek waiting at my car. I still have no idea how he found me. I had barely reached him in the parking lot when his fist broke my nose and I fell on my knees. He spat, "Get up, b**ch we haven't even started." He told me we were getting married. He wanted to make sure I couldn't leave again.

We picked up his little daughter and went to the store to get her a dress for the wedding, my nose still bandaged up. He had connections to the Mexican mob, and brought their priest to marry us. When I hesitated on my vows, I was met with a handgun. I got married at gunpoint.

He cut me off from my family and my friends. He logged into my IM account and told them hurtful things pretending to be me. I could watch the conversations, but was powerless to stop him. I didn't want them to get hurt.

The next two years is still a blur. He beat me every week, and don't get me wrong, I fought back ... but meth addicts don't feel. I gained weight so he couldn't throw me around (and hoped he would leave me alone). I tried to leave. I had a friend sign for my apartment and took a cab. He beat the cab driver until he got my address.

He took me to Hawaii for my birthday and when I didn't feel like going out to party he left me in our hotel room and brought a hooker back to our bed while I tried to sleep.

**He was so cruel.**

I remember being chained to a radiator. I can't count how many times he raped me.

I've had 14 facial reconstruction surgeries. I can show you the dent where he shot me in the face. I can show you where the bullets went in when he shot me in the stomach. He took me to his mob doctors. They'd stitch me up and send me back home with him.

All that time he was setting up fraudulent companies in my family's name, and borrowed upwards of 250K in their name.

One day in 2006, after a particularly rough night of fighting, the police came and arrested my husband. I'm still not sure who turned him in but I was overwhelmingly grateful. I tried to turn him in many times–within hours they'd bring him back. Something was different that day. I didn't know if he would be back, but I knew I couldn't take much more.

After a few short weeks of visiting him in prison to make sure he was really gone, I started to put my life back together. Due to the damage done to the door by the police, my husband's criminal record, his failure to report to probation, and the fact that he wasn't on the lease, my landlord gave me two weeks to get out. I was evicted for my 5th time in two years.

I was fortunate enough to have started a temp job working with the Arizona Department of Economic Security and I loved it.

Somehow, I managed to keep my home troubles somewhat out of the office. I had a decent income but no place to stay.

I ran into one of Derek's friends, who offered to help me move out. Derek owed him money, but of course I didn't know that. True to his word, he did help me transfer things into storage, but sold some of our furniture to the mother of his five children, pocketing half of the money and taking half of my stuff. This was after he took my car, dropped me off at work, and then disappeared. I eventually got the car back, but not for a year.

**In July 2007, I was homeless.**

The first night, I stayed at work until the office closed. I hung out at the library until it closed too. Then I found myself under a bridge just around the corner. I had only my keepsakes, like my son's birth certificate and my phone.

For three months I spent my nights under that bridge. For the first time in my life, no one bothered me. I was completely free ... independent. Most people would look at homelessness as the low point of their life. I had just been freed of mine. Ironically, at work I was writing contracts benefiting the homeless and victims of domestic violence, as well as aging and hunger. I loved helping the state wrap around these communities, and I never told anyone at work what I experienced. My supervisor, Cam, was such an independent and fierce woman—I gravitated towards her and learned what a healthy life could look like.

During the day, I would book conference rooms at work to sleep. At night, I would play games on my phone and listen to the homeless man who lived 100 feet to my right. We never acknowledged each other, and I couldn't really see him through his shopping cart fort ... but I could hear him singing. Every night he would sing "Ooh Child" by the Five Stairsteps about how things would get easier and brighter some day.

I don't know if my dad would sing me that song but it certainly feels like he did. I knew that this man was my guardian angel—a messenger from my father. I never got a chance to thank Singing Sam (as I named him), but this stranger who spoke not one word to me ... gave me hope again.

I finally called my mom and told her I needed her, though I didn't even have to say the words. She offered immediately, "Baby, come home."

After being with my mom for six months, I started getting back on my feet. Over the next few years, I moved in with several roommates, petitioned to see my son again, lost in court, and casually dated. I got married again and divorced again.

I wanted so badly to be with Aerick, but I didn't know how to be a mom. James had already found another woman, and she really cared for my son. Aerick had already been through so much, and I didn't want more traumas for his life, so I opted for a smaller role. James and his new woman were raising him right, so I saw him on special occasions.

Derek, my first husband, got out one time and called my work to threaten me. He threatened one of my coworkers instead and went back to prison for threatening a State employee. I stayed at that job until I knew he was away for good. I loved the extra layer of protection that job afforded me.

**Over time, my fears lessened.**

In 2015, I met my soulmate on Craigslist. My life has never been the same. Even through the battles and our demons, we complement each other's strengths and weaknesses. He's a force, like I am, but he fights for me. Yes, we've struggled to find common ground, but we click and connect in ways that I never thought possible. I now know what love is, and what it's not.

I've reconnected with my son, who has graduated and is every bit my heart as he ever was. I'm so incredibly proud of the man he grew up to be.

With the love and support of my man, in 2017, I quit the family business and once again followed my father's entrepreneurial spirit. I became a professional organizer–my true calling. My mother confirmed that as a child I would reorganize my room every week. I think it made me feel that I could create order in the chaos. People should always know they have choices.

It's interesting: the biggest reason people live in their mess is because they're embarrassed to allow anyone into it. And believe me, I get that. People I loved were shut out of my life to protect them and to protect myself. But do you know what I've learned in my 100 lifetimes?

**Some people are kind.**

You have to trust to find out.

That's the power of people: needing, wanting, and helping people. I changed my name back to Aislinn. I've reclaimed my dreamer personality. It's far more rewarding than I could have imagined.

Now, people respect me for my feelings, needs, strengths, and weaknesses. I control my life—whom I let in or keep out. It feels good to be understood. I feel so seen now, not just by people but by God. I didn't know he was there before.

I used to be terrified to make myself vulnerable again, but speaking hard truths is a part of life ... and it's safe now. I'm open with the thoughts in my head and the feelings in my heart.

For most of my life, I felt like I didn't exist. All people saw when they looked at me was a cute pair of legs, nice eyes or some great cheekbones, and I thought that was all there was. Happy, sad, and mad were the only emotions I knew.

But, you know what? I am strong. I am resilient. I am a survivor. And yes, I'm still giving myself time to heal.

I realize mine is not the worst story, some of my friends have been through worse. But I am willing to share mine with you. To the readers who have been through similar experiences, or are going through them now, just like Singing Sam taught me, it gets better and brighter days are ahead. Just hold on.

# Alicia Miyares Laszewski

**Founder of Brand Ethos**

*H*eart Word: Be Brave / Life will come at you in many shapes and forms. Fear will too. If you are Brave and have Faith, you can step through anything and come out stronger on the other side of anything that comes your way.

Alicia Laszewski is the Founder of Brand Ethos, a Communications & Branding firm. In 2018, she bravely elected to do a proactive double mastectomy after doctors uncovered suspicious cell development that could be taking her down a rough path. She took this courage as fuel to reengineer her life personally and professionally after the medical journey.

Her professional career spans a variety of roles including Global Chief Marketing Officer for a Singapore-based customer experience firm, Broward County Chapter Executive and Regional Marketing Officer for the American Red Cross, and other Vice President-level roles.

Alicia and her husband, Kory, reside in Florida with their children Austin, Ana Sofia, Kory Jr., and Konnor. She's an active volunteer at school and shuttles them to sports and activities while balancing her work and spiritual life.

Born and raised in Spartanburg, South Carolina, Alicia received her BS in Marketing and Communications from Clemson University.

# Facing My Biggest Fear

## By Alicia Laszewski

When I went in to get my double mastectomy, friends and family commented on how I made it appear like I was heading to the salon for a pedicure. From the perspective of an outsider looking in, that is probably what it looked like, but there is so much more to the story.

Let me start by sharing a little bit about my family and upbringing. I was born and raised in Spartanburg, South Carolina. My family is originally from Cuba, but my dad left for Clemson University in Clemson, South Carolina, where he studied engineering. He went back to Cuba to get my mom, where they got married not too long after he graduated in 1959. Eventually, they ended up in Spartanburg, South Carolina, to plant roots and raise a family.

My maternal grandparents were from Valladolid, Spain, and my paternal grandfather was born in Key West, Florida, something he told me every time we spoke. All my grandparents were thankful for the opportunity to come to America. My cousins were sprinkled between Miami and Puerto Rico, and my parents made sure to keep us connected to not only our grandparents, but to our amazing aunts, uncles, and cousins. What a blessing that proved to be.

It felt like we were the only Spanish-speaking families in South Carolina. Out of us three kids, I was the youngest as my brother is ten years older than me and my sister is eight-and-a-half years older than me. Sometimes, I say that I have two sets of parents because my brother and sister are amazing mentors and humans in addition to my hardworking parents. As they both got married,

I kept gaining parents. My sister-in-law, Theresa, and brother-in-law, Gonzalo, stepped into those roles nicely!

So, there we were, Cubans from South Carolina. I'm perfectly bilingual even though I have a very strong southern accent which is oftentimes confusing for others. I'm also Catholic, which is rare in South Carolina. I went to Catholic school until sixth grade and played tennis and loved all sports. My parents taught us the importance of serving not only our parish community, but outside the church, too. My mom volunteered for a charitable organization called T.O.T.A.L. Ministries, which taught me the importance of giving back.

After graduating from Clemson University, I moved to Miami to work for WLTV-23, a television station. Although I had been to Miami multiple times throughout my life, this was my first time living in the big city away from my parents who were, and continue to be, an important part of my life.

My sister, Ani, already lived in Miami with her husband and 1-year-old daughter. Their lives as working parents were so busy, but they always found time to take care of me. My Aunt Tia Chiqui was a divorced, empty nester, so she stepped in as my Miami mom.

**History wasn't going to repeat itself with me.**

I was always fearful of being diagnosed with breast cancer. Even mammograms freaked me out. And there was a good reason. When I was in my 20s, I watched my Aunt Tia Chiqui—one of my most favorite people on earth—die of breast cancer. She was diagnosed on February 18th, 2000, which was ironically on her 56th birthday. She was one of the bravest people I've ever known, and we shared a special connection. In the final days of hospice care at my Aunt Lourdes' home, I remember praying for my Miami mom to die to get her out of her misery, and at the same time praying for a miracle, too. There is nothing worse than seeing someone you love and admire so much succumb to cancer so rapidly. She died on November 9th—nearly nine months later.

It was surreal for every person in our family to have her gone. As my mom's side of the family gathered for the funeral, my dad's side of the family—my aunt, uncle, and cousins—stood right alongside them. I don't think I fully realized the blessing this was to be surrounded by so much love. I just knew I had to be strong for my cousins. I knew that as horrible as I felt that day, she was my aunt, but she was their mom.

That's when the fear started. The bravery came much later. I was dating my husband, Kory, when she died. I immediately became active in Gilda's Club of South Florida where I met so many wonderful lifelong friends that to this day, I consider family. I coped with her loss by finding a way to raise money and make positive changes for families living with cancer. At this point in my career, I had left working in television. I was now embarking on a strong corporate path that led me to become a vice president before age 30. I had fundraising and event planning skills and was not afraid to do the hard work for those living with cancer. Doing that gave me incredible purpose and healing during a period of incredible loss.

**Life goes on.**

After my Aunt Tia Chiqui died, I wondered if I should start doing mammograms. I was only 29. Although her cancer was not heredi-tary, I was cautious. My OB/GYN, Jose, is married to my cousin, Maria, who happens to be a breast radiologist. We really like to keep it all in the family! In my early 30s, the annual mammograms began.

From that point on, my parents, husband, or my close friend had to go with me when I went for a mammogram. That's the level of incredible fear and anxiety I had about cancer. I would only go for a mammogram if my cousin Maria was there to read the images. The stress would start and simmer a week or two before my appointment. While I'm a go-getter, independent, and self-sufficient, when it comes to the topic of breast cancer, I become a real mess FAST. I knew if I ever had cancer, I'd need to be brave just like my Aunt Tia Chiqui.

The fears grew stronger after I had children. In 2002, Kory and I married, and I became the stepmother to his son, Austin. Kory, Jr. was born in 2004, Ana Sofia in 2008, and little Konnor in 2012. In 2015, my son Austin brought his friend Alex home from football, and he is a special part of our family to this day.

Each of my biological children were premature babies. Ana Sofia and Konnor each spent some time in the NICU after some dramatic C-sections. I reflect on that time and cannot believe how brave I was. I became like a frail child in the waiting room of a mammogram, yet I was like a fearless tiger sitting next to my children in the NICU.

**Waiting for the other shoe to drop.**

About five years ago, my parents called asking me to pray for my cousin. My sometimes-emotional father delivers news like a non-emotional reporter—he gets to the point fast. He told me that my cousin Maria had just come out of surgery for breast cancer. She kept it all private until after she endured the surgery. Although it was cancer, it was the best of all possible outcomes, and they performed the double mastectomy that day with no treatment needed.

I fell to my knees and literally lost my breath when I heard this news. First Chiqui, and now the person who was the breast cancer prevention specialist in my life actually HAD breast cancer. If she could get it, I could too even with the best preventative care. How could this even be possible knowing that she got her regular mammograms? Wow, that was scary, and it was a mental game-changer for me.

When I went in for my routine mammogram in July 2018, something wasn't quite right. An ultrasound followed the mammogram. Maria told me not to worry or cry, but they needed to do a biopsy similar to the one they did back in 2009, which turned out to be nothing. This felt different. She looked at me and said, "No matter what, we kick cancer's butt all the time. Have faith."

I'm not sure why, but I could never fully believe her. My husband and parents would say to me, "If Maria isn't worried, then why are you?" As rational as that sounds, the irrational mind and voice are so much louder, and mine is downright boisterous.

The biopsy came back abnormal and noted I had ADH cells. I was at lunch with my husband and one of his business partners, and stepped outside to take the call. Oh, how I cried! She explained that ADH cells are like changing cells that were not cancer but needed to be removed. She set up an appointment with her surgeon—the best oncology surgeon in the hospital. I fell apart.

I saw the surgeon about a week later. My mom and Kory went with me. She explained that we would be scheduling a surgery to remove the tissue where the cells were found and biopsy the entire area because sometimes cancer could be near the biopsy location. She also needed to schedule an MRI. I fell apart again, what if they find something new on the MRI? How could I possibly endure waiting until August 28th for my surgery date?

Then that voice started again—the loud, irrational one. "Why does this doctor want to do the MRI? I bet she feels like the other scans missed something and she's looking for the really bad stuff."

At the same time, my sister was told she had cancer on her tongue. This really could not be happening.

At this point, it was late July. I was freaking out because we had planned a cruise with the entire family. I had to decide whether to cancel or not. After about a day, the switch flipped. I told Kory that if the MRI didn't show anything scary, we were going on our cruise. My mother sat in my appointment with the surgeon, knowing that my sister was officially getting the news about her cancer, and did not say a WORD to me. She didn't crack at all. That's brave and strong.

The MRI did not show anything new, so we went on the week-long cruise. I enjoyed every moment with my family exactly as I should have. I created my prayer circle, and one special person told me that God was maybe trying to tell me to, "Slow down my computer." I stored that one away, but it came full circle.

I came back to my birthday celebration, the first day of school, and surgery. The Friday before Labor Day, four days after surgery, I got the call. It was Maria. She was calm and wanted to let me know they didn't find cancer in the tissue, but they did find LCIS tissue which is known to be a marker for cancer. My risk had gone up. After meeting with my surgeon, I learned that I had two choices:

1. Take the drug, tamoxifen, used to help lower the risk of breast cancer in women who are considered high risk and have check-ups every six months to monitor the breasts. They will alternate between a mammogram/ultrasound and an MRI.

2. Have a prophylactic double mastectomy.

I asked, "What if I choose to do nothing?" The response was simple: doing nothing was not an option.

The night that I received the news, we went out to dinner as a family to celebrate. Yes, celebrate. I know that must sound strange and bizarre, but I had to focus on something positive and get my family focused on the same thing. I did not HAVE cancer. The pathology may not have been squeaky clean, but it COULD have been way worse. My mindset started to shift from falling apart to becoming a warrior.

In mid-September, we met the oncologist to discuss it all in more detail. My surgeon suggested that I meet with everyone on the team and make an informed decision, which was the absolute best advice.

As my husband and I were leaving the office, he asked me, "Which way are you leaning?" I said, "I don't know. You know, we have Kory, Jr.'s Confirmation in October, and I don't want to ruin that. So, I think I'll eventually do the mastectomy, but maybe I'll do the tamoxifen first so that everyone can enjoy the holidays and we'll operate in January."

That's when he looked into my eyes and said, "Look, I'm not trying to tell you what to do, but I've researched tamoxifen. And I know you. Each time you have a mammogram, we lose a few weeks of you because you start panicking in the weeks leading up to it. The anxiety paralyzes you. Then, God forbid, if it turns into a biopsy or a second look, we lose a few more weeks of you after. That means if you are going to get checked every six months, we're going to lose you four out of every six months of the year."

First of all, he's smart. That's why I married him. I responded, "Well, that's a very good point. I worry. And I don't really love taking medication either." My oncologist shared that the tamoxifen would reduce my risk of breast cancer by 50 percent compared to a mastectomy that would reduce my risk by over 90 percent. My risk had gone up from the one in eight that all women have to roughly a 25-30 percent chance of getting cancer. He also shared that if I waited until January, I would have to be re-scanned all over again to be sure nothing new was brewing.

**I opted for the immediate double mastectomy.**

To finalize my decision, I met with the plastic surgeon, and I felt a God-wink, as one of my buddies says. The plastic surgeon happened to be a Cuban from North Carolina. What were the odds? Both he and the breast oncology surgeon were available the week after Kory's confirmation, November 5th, so the stars were aligning. Another God-wink.

After the meeting, I decided on the spot to go for the double mastectomy, and there was no turning back in my mind. My sister was well into her recovery and healing from her tongue cancer (THANK GOD!), and now it was my turn to be the big girl.

Then, it dawned on me that I would be having this surgery the week of Tia Chiqui's passing anniversary. She would be my guardian angel. One of my friends sent me a card that simply stated, "Be Brave." All of this clicked at that moment, and I knew that I didn't want my children to lose their mom young. I refocused my thinking around gratitude. So many women had died of breast cancer—like my aunt. How many of them would have gladly opted for a PROACTIVE double mastectomy if it would have spared them the pain and suffering? I knew I had to be strong and brave to show my four boys, and ESPECIALLY my daughter, what it was like to go through adversity and come out the other side—making lemonade out of lemons.

When I talked to the surgeon before the surgery, I said, "Just take 'em! But, please don't let me flatline on the table." That was my biggest, most haunting fear of all—flatlining.

My aunt was there in spirit, guiding me through the process and helping me be brave. My prayer warriors comprised of my family and friends from around the world who were right there with me—and I felt it. I tried to sneak in a rock, blessed by our parish priest, into the surgery with me because without faith, there was no such thing as bravery. Kory confiscated it before they took me back, and had it right there waiting for me next to my "Be Brave" card alongside my hospital bed in recovery.

The five-hour surgery was a breeze for me and, no, I didn't flatline. For my husband, sister, and parents in the waiting room, five hours felt like five days. For my brother and sister-in-law in South Carolina, and my sweet nieces and nephews all over the country, it may have felt even longer. My cousin Gloria, Chiqui's only daughter, earned the job of babysitter for my kids who were so distracted by the sleepover with her that they didn't have time to worry about me.

A few days after the surgery, I was feeling great. The drains were not fun, but I made it through the entire recovery with just Advil and a muscle relaxer—zero narcotic pain meds were needed. However, the pathology report showed that my fears were justified. They found Stage 0 DCIS tissue which means in a very dense part of the nipple, there was Stage 0 cancer.

**When bravery is contagious.**

During my recovery, I jumped back into family life as a wife and working mother. My busy job as a global chief marketing officer became all-consuming, and I needed to make some adjustments so I could be there for my family. The things I tolerated from my professional life were quickly becoming unacceptable. Three weeks after surgery, I gave my 90-day notice to my employer, hired a life coach, and started working on building my own company. God gave me a chance to live this life, and I was going to do it my way.

We had a few bumps in the road, which delayed my dream of starting my own marketing and consulting company. Fear slowly crept back into my mind. But in the end, I realized that the only way to really "slow down my computer" was to leap from my comfort zone. I chose to work with people, companies, and organizations that were meaningful to me. I wanted to make a difference in the lives of small to mid-size business owners and see brands grow and flourish. I wanted my own little Lemonade Stand!

I was being recruited by companies which would be the safe route, or I could just rip off the band aid and build my own firm. I chose the brave route because deep down, I knew that I COULD do it.

I named the firm, Brand Ethos, and I'm so proud to say my little company is thriving! I am surrounded by an amazing team of people who share the same ethics, morals, and values that I do. We are working with fantastic clients and growing our portfolio weekly.

**Take a leap of faith.**

I am not that special or unique. I might be high energy, have an amazing family that supports me, and have had a great career on paper. Still, so many other women—all the women in this book—are special! The greatest accomplishments in life are based upon the impact we make on others. My Catholic faith calls for me to live that through the Golden Rule; to treat others as we want to be treated. Some days I do a better job at it than others, but this journey that I just shared with you has taken me to the point of such clarity that I hope you can learn from it, too.

Count your blessings always. My biggest blessings are my family—the immediate and extended family that God has given me—and my health. And when you have that, pay it forward!

With your blessings counted, create a life that helps you focus on that. If you can create your own company, do it. If you can find a company to work for that honors family and balance, work there! Don't settle is my point because you can do it if you are BRAVE.

**It's okay to be afraid. Be brave.**

Because of what I've gone through, I've had to face fear head on. The fear will always be there, but I'm finding my way around it. When it came to my double mastectomy, I treated it like I treat everything in my life. I was afraid, but I wasn't going to hide. I needed to be brave enough to be proactive in doing something about it before it got me like it did my aunt and so many other amazing women we've lost to this disease. I wasn't caught up in how I would look afterwards.

I feel great today thanks to some amazing surgeons and a super special radiologist who will forever hold a special place in my heart. Maria has told me that each day on her ride to work, she prays that God gives her the eyes to read the scans to save people's lives. I encourage everyone to pray for every doctor to have those eyes.

I used to be so afraid of cancer and what it could do to me or my family. I would be lying if I said it did not scare me. My close friends will tell you that I get triggered by fear pretty easily. But the blessing we have today is that we can get preventative screenings and have access to the data, which allows us to make informed decisions—like choosing to do a proactive mastectomy.

Do not read my story and think I am glamorizing the mastectomy because that could not be further from the truth. Here's my message: this world is filled with brilliant minds who have used their talents to find screenings and tests that allow us to get ahead of stuff. We also have doctors with great eyes and brains to make a lifesaving impact. This is fuel for bravery.

Don't be afraid of mammograms because they can save your life. Don't be afraid of starting your own business or leaving a toxic job, because that too can save your life. It's okay to be afraid. But, if you can be afraid AND be brave, you, my dear, can do anything you want in this world. Believe it because I believe in you.

# Davina Lyons

**Educator, Speaker, Purpose Coach
and Founder of Tribe Authentic Woman**

*H*eart Word: Authentic / I believe that everyone should live according to their core values and what they are passionate about—that is their authentic self. There is so much more I could say since my entire business platform is based upon the word authentic and what it means to live an authentic life.

Davina Lyons teaches 7th and 8th grade English Language Arts at Sacaton Middle School in the Gila River Indian Community in Sacaton, AZ. She completed her bachelor's degree in Business Management and her Master's in Management with an emphasis on Transformational Leadership. Before becoming a teacher, Lyons spent 29 years in corporate America as a people and project leader. In 2014, Lyons followed her passion for learning and inspiring others and decided to become an educator. She was quickly able to build authentic, compassionate relationships with her students which created a positive classroom environment. She created a classroom brand called "The Lyons Den" which inspired students to feel connected and fostered a sense of pride in the school community. After seeing untapped potential in many students, Lyons started a theater club where she is teaching students to write, produce and act in their own plays.

In addition to her work in the classroom, she desires to support adolescents in navigating through social and emotional barriers to more fully engage academically. She is the founder of the TRIBE Authentic Woman Workshop where she inspires and motivates women to discover their true self, learn to walk and talk in alignment with their core values, and live their truth unapologetically. She currently resides in Chandler, AZ.

# Becoming a Tribe Authentic Woman

## By Davina Lyons

I felt like a burden even before I was born. Despite not being wanted, I was born in New Haven, Connecticut, on November 3rd, 1964. At age 20, my mother, Gwen, met my father, Tony, in a nightclub. I was conceived after a brief sexual encounter. When my mother was eight months pregnant, my father shoved her, and she called the police. At that moment, he decided he wanted nothing to do with her. By the time I was born, my father was in jail.

A hospital social worker convinced my mother to keep me, declaring it would be a mistake to give me up for adoption because one day, she would be proud of me. For some reason, she listened, although she never showed me any love or affection.

Ironically, the number one song in the US Top Ten that year was "Baby Love" by the Supremes. My mother remembers there was a lot of talk about politics and voting on the day of my birth. It was a significant and progressive time in US history and it was an election year. Lyndon Johnson (Democrat) defeated Barry Goldwater (Republican) for US President. Additionally, Washington, D.C. residents were able to vote in a presidential election for the first time.

The social worker brought my mother and me to her home straight from the hospital. For the first couple of weeks of my life, she taught my mother the basics of newborn care. With the help of the Department of Social Services (DES), my mom got an apartment. The rent was $99 a month, and she received $100, plus food stamps. I imagine it was really tough for my mother, a naive girl fresh out of the south, rejected by her mother and raised by her grandparents.

My mother came to New Haven from North Carolina in search of her mother, Jean (my grandmother). Jean abandoned her and her sister, and left the state long ago. My mom was just 4 when Jean left her abusive husband and the girls behind in search of a better life. After she left, my mom went to live with her grandparents while an aunt raised her sister.

My mom grew up feeling unloved and unwanted by her family as she looked like her abusive father. In contrast, her sister was brought up in a loving home and showered with gifts, including a brand-new car and a fur coat for high school graduation. Yet, my mother was determined to find her mom in New Haven and have a relationship. When she finally found her, she was living with a very young man (only a few years older than my mother).

When I was six months old, she met and married her first husband, Junior. He was smitten with my mother's beauty and did not mind being a father. He took me everywhere, and as a small child, I looked up to him. He was my "daddy." In fact, I didn't realize he wasn't my biological father until the fifth grade. When I was about 8, a tall, handsome man with a deep voice approached me and my mother. He leaned down and said, "Look at this pretty little girl."

You could feel the tension as he took a $5 bill out of his wallet and tried to give it to me. My mother said, "No," and gave it back to him. Junior was in the store and asked my biological father to leave. He turned and walked away. When we got to the car, my mom and Junior argued. Junior said, "You should have told her he was her uncle." It was like they didn't know I was sitting there in the back seat. I knew it was a lie right away. I wanted to ask, "What uncle? I had one aunt. How did this stranger all of a sudden become my uncle?" Later, I heard my mom tell someone at the store that Junior acted like a fool when they saw Tony at the store. That's when I knew Junior was not my dad.

From the very beginning, Junior was violent towards my mother and strict with me. He abused alcohol and drugs, and was an extreme womanizer. My mother and I experienced domestic violence on a regular basis. He broke her jaw, and she was hospitalized a few times—yet, she would forgive him, and everything would be fine in a day or two. I grew accustomed to waking up in the middle of the night to yelling and screaming, or the police arresting him for attacking her again.

My mother wasted no words with me and was a strict disciplinarian. Although she drank alcohol daily, especially in my formative years, she made sure the house was clean, proper meals were cooked, and I had what I needed for school. In fact, from the outside looking in, our home appeared neat and tidy. If it wasn't for the men she chose, like Junior, and the fact that she was incapable of outwardly expressing love, she could have been a pretty good mom. At one point, because I always felt like a burden, I asked my mother if she ever loved me. She responded, "What is love? Does it exist? What does that look like? No one ever showed that to me." I recall overhearing her tell someone she was really upset with, a cousin who had once had an abortion, that she wouldn't help her abort me. She explained she would have, but she was too far along. One thing was clear—I would forever be a burden to her.

One night, I was sent by my mother to tag along with Junior. Junior's older brother had just bought a brand new red 1969 Ford Mustang Mach 1. I rode in the back seat while they were drinking, driving, and yelling out the car window to God knows who— showing off. Finally, they pulled into a parking lot. There was a bright streetlight shining into the car. I heard an argument between Junior and some stranger. It became pretty intense. I couldn't really see what was happening from the back seat. That's when the passenger side door slung open wide, and Junior climbed into the back seat on top of me. I then saw why he was so frantic. The man he was arguing with had a razor (a sharp blade) slicing the air with the intent to cut him. When the man realized I was in the car, he stopped. I remember how close that blade came to slicing my face. Junior made me promise not to tell my mother about the incident.

When I was in the third grade, the police showed up to answer a neighbor's call; my friends and I scattered around the block. I'm not sure why I decided to double back, but I did. I vividly remember attempting to climb into the driver's side window of the police car parked in the middle of the street. I was almost in! Suddenly, my entire body was snatched out from the window and carried like a sack of potatoes over Junior's shoulder, headed toward our house. We took the route through the backyard past a row of bushes. Junior reached for a branch off one of the bushes while successfully balancing me on his shoulders. Before I knew it, I was being whipped. He hit my bare legs and behind with a force that I'll never forget.

When my mom came home, I was sitting in a kitchen chair with blood oozing from my legs. There were a gazillion tiny pinholes. In his rage, Junior failed to realize the branch he grabbed was from a thorny rose bush. This was the second time in my life I remember my mother coming to my rescue or defending me after the damage had been done. She genuinely felt sorry for me.

The most unforgettable memory that haunts me even today, happened that same year. Gwen and Junior hosted a party in our home. Of course, I was sent to bed at a certain time and could only hear the music and noise of the party. I eventually drifted off to sleep. At some point, in the middle of the night, I was awakened by loud screams and objects breaking and crashing. I got up and peaked out into the living room area and saw Junior choking my mother. She couldn't breathe!

I ran and leaped on his back. He flung me off to the sofa without hesitation. I didn't give up! I did it again until he let her go. He was cursing and asking her, "Where is it?" I did not know what "it" was at the time. Later, I found out she removed the spark plug wires from the car to keep him from leaving the party, following some woman he was fixated on. She hid those wires, and the car was dead. After more hitting and choking, she relinquished the wires. To prevent her from calling the police, he took the phone cord from the wall outlet and left.

At this point, my mom and I set out to find a telephone to call the police. We were both in our nighttime clothes and desperate to get help before he returned. We walked through the neighborhood looking for a home with the lights on. Down the block, there was an apartment building. We knocked on a door where there were several people partying who let us in. They motioned us towards a phone on the wall in a hallway. They were young—perhaps teens or young adults. They were teasing me in a playful, half-mean way, while my mom was on the phone. A couple of them laughed as my mom was still gasping for air while talking. I stood there with my arms folded, wishing I had superhero powers to end this nightmare. The next day, they were back together again.

Gwen and Junior divorced when I was in the sixth grade. Finally, she had enough. It took courage and a chunk of her soul to walk away from that relationship. I was at my Grandmother Jean's house when my mother came to pick me up. She had a tiny suitcase for me and a much larger one for her. She offered no explanation because I was a child and children were to be "seen and not heard." I could only listen to my mother and grandmother plotting our escape. A large black car picked us up. It seemed we drove forever, but eventually, we ended up at the Kennedy LaGuardia Airport in New York and boarded an airplane for an unknown destination.

I had a million thoughts. I had so many questions that I was afraid to ask for fear of being scolded. Where were we going? Where was my dog, Major? Why didn't she grab my favorite doll? Where is Junior? Is he mad? Will I see my friends again? I needed to know so much. Our plane landed at the Seattle-Tacoma Airport (SeaTac) late at night. There to greet us was Aunt Joyce, Uncle Roy, and my baby cousins whom I had never met in person. Chapter Two of my life was about to begin—it was October of 1975.

## Chapter Two

While I was in sixth grade, I attended three elementary schools during that first school year in Washington State. We moved around quite a bit until my mother met a man named Gilbert. At the time, she was a receptionist at a combination used car dealership and shady motel setup (think fleabag motel). Gilbert's cousin lived in one of the units of the motel and wanted to point out the new gal working in the front office to Gilbert. I was there when she met him as I was out of school for the summer. He immediately began calling in the evenings and taking her out for dinner. He was clearly different from Junior in every way. He creeped me out for some reason. I told my mother I did not like him, but she dismissed it as jealousy on my part.

My mother had come from a family with money and property in North Carolina. But, when her mother, Jean, abandoned her, our family was taken out of the family inheritance. Most importantly to her, Gilbert owned real estate and had plenty of money in the bank. I imagined she thought it would be different and that finally, her life would be changed for the better. Despite others warning her that he was a monster, she ignored it. He provided the security that she craved. I was too young to make sense of it all, but I knew something wasn't right.

Like my mother, I enjoyed the perks of their relationship. One day, while she was at an appointment, he offered to take me shopping. We went to the mall, and he basically told me I could have anything I wanted. That day, I had the second hole in my ears pierced, got a new bicycle, a host of clothes, and costume jewelry. It was an amazing day, but it came with a price.

One Saturday morning, I was sitting on the floor close to the television, watching my favorite series of cartoons. Gilbert was sitting behind me on the couch. My mother was in the kitchen cooking breakfast. He said, "Why are you down there? Come sit next to me on the couch." He patted the seat where I was to sit and without thinking, I complied. It was innocent on my part, but he was grooming me. I had no clue. I was 12 years old. That was the beginning of something that I wished could have been erased for many years to come. The guilt and shame associated with the trauma of molestation is unbelievable. I was never the same.

The seventh grade was pivotal for me. Since I was experiencing the unspeakable at home, I couldn't tell anyone. My mother loved her home and the car she was privileged to drive. I did not want to disrupt her elevated status. I was the kid she did not want. My mere existence was a burden, so I kept my mouth shut.

She wasn't happy, though and she began to drink more. Gilbert had become violent and aggressive with her, just like Junior. So, I struck a deal with him. If he would be nicer to her and tolerate her drinking, I would cooperate with him. From ages 12 to 15, that is what I did behind closed doors. Meanwhile, I wore a mask at school and worked hard to prove that I was not like the garbage I felt like inside.

I signed up to perform in the school talent show that year. For some reason, I chose singing as my talent. Ironically, I sang, "Killing Me Softly" by Roberta Flack.

I stepped out on the stage, and the instrumental track began to play. As I began singing, someone yelled from the audience, "You are killing me softly with your singing!" Instead of continuing to sing, I froze. Something within me snapped! For the first time ever, I spoke up for myself. The background music halted. I put my left hand on my hip and began to deliver a speech chastising the person who had the nerve to rudely insult me. The theme of my extemporaneous speech was courage. I had the courage to get up there, and that person was a coward in the audience for bullying me. I never knew who actually said it, but I loved the feeling of commanding the audience.

Immediately following the talent show, I was approached by Mr. H. R. Thomas, a community activist, who took a special interest in volunteering and working with school children in the community. His nickname was Rock; I thought that was pretty cool. He asked me if I liked to speak. I said, I guess so, not really understanding his question. He told me about an oratorical competition coming up and encouraged me to prepare an eight to ten-minute speech on the topic of my choice.

At that time, The Equal Rights Amendment was a big deal. Although Congress passed the amendment in March of 1972, there were still several states yet to ratify it. I chose this topic for my first speech competition. At age 12, I knew nothing about the broader perspectives of women's rights. However, I did know that my rights were being violated on every level. I froze during that speech and placed last in the competition. I ran off crying to the basement of the church where the competition was being held.

A lady I did not know followed me. She spoke gently and expressed the importance of not giving up. She told me to hold my head high and go back upstairs. At that point, I listened, and I am so glad I did. In the very next local competition, I took first place. From there, I achieved another first-place victory in a

State Competition, which led me to the Regional Competition in Stockton, CA, where I placed first again. I went to the Nationals in Chicago, Illinois, where I was coached not to be so dramatic and passionate because it was frowned upon at that level. The guy who took first place demonstrated so much passion that he actually leaped off the stage like a leopard into the audience. That taught me a lesson.

Speaking was empowering for me. All the while, I was still wearing the mask and hiding the abuse at home from my mother and the world. My mother obviously suspected something was happening between Gilbert and I, but did not want to face it. During my freshman year in high school, she confronted me because she thought I was being flirtatious and told me to stay out of his face. She blamed me. I never wanted to be alone with him and would ask to go with her if she was leaving the house. I was devastated that she turned on me. She saw me only as the burden I was. So, I packed my suitcase and walked. On my way out the door, she said, "Walk down the alley instead of the street, so the neighbors don't see you." I complied. I had not made it very far when the police rolled up on me. It was illegal for juveniles to run away at that time.

I was interrogated for hours at the police station about why I was running away. Finally, I told them everything. That night, I was taken to a "receiving home." So much more happened after this. Gilbert filed for divorce immediately. The judge ordered he give my mother enough money to start over in an apartment. I moved in with her. My mother attempted suicide multiple times when I was a child living in Connecticut. She attempted suicide two more times—the following Christmas Eve and the next year while I was a senior in high school. Eventually, she left me alone in the apartment and returned to Gilbert. She told me it was my responsibility to figure out where I was going to live once the apartment lease ended in about a month.

None of my friend's parents would take me in, and my aunt, uncle, and cousins lived too far away. I had nowhere to go. I quietly went back to live with Gilbert and Gwen. Nothing was said between Gilbert and me. He avoided me at all costs. I managed to negotiate my own telephone line in my bedroom, a small television, and a stereo. I only ate in my room and never stayed in the same room with either of them. I graduated from high school with honors and attended The Evergreen State College in Olympia, WA. They both helped me move out. I was happy to finally be free.

## Repeating the Cycle

I was ill-equipped and too damaged to make the kind of choices I needed to make. Because I didn't know any better, I repeated the cycle of my mother and grandmother. Rock, the community activist, who I admired so much, warned me to focus on my education and stay on track. I did not listen. I got married to Prentiss my freshman year of college, and had my first miscarriage at the end of my second year. It was 1984. I was 24 weeks pregnant. I was traumatized. From there, I moved to Arizona. Two years later, I lost my second baby at 20-plus weeks, and two years after that, it happened again.

Nine years later, in another relationship, I lost my fourth baby in the same way, and that same year, I had a first-trimester loss. I lost five babies in total. I had uterine fibroids that grew exponentially. Every month I hemorrhaged to the point of severe anemia. I gained weight with each pregnancy that I seemed to never lose. The first marriage ended due to infidelity on his part. Since he and I started dating when I was 16, and we divorced at 27, I was naive and vulnerable to whatever a guy said. I followed the same negative patterns as my mother and fell deeper into despair.

My credit was ruined by the first miscarriage, and because we had no health insurance, we left the hospital with no baby and a $13,000 bill. I was young and impulsive with my money. In fact, it was difficult to reason with me most days because I was so angry about how my life turned out. My relationship with my mother was disastrous. We went years without speaking. I was angry because she chose Gilbert's annual Carpenter's Picnic over my wedding. My mother was never there for anything I did. Every award I received, every speech I gave, even when I became the Queen of Pageant, she was nowhere to be found. I was a chore for her.

I never did successfully deliver a viable child. It hurt. I blamed myself and for years believed that it was punishment for what happened with my stepfather, Gilbert. By becoming more religious and asking God's forgiveness, I finally overcame that notion. I also adopted a son, who was my first cousin's son, Jordan Seth, when he was eight months old. He will always be the BEST decision I ever made. Through him, I finally understood unconditional love. My second best decision was becoming a teacher in the Gila River Indian Community in Sacaton, Arizona.

I was once told that I would one day be a "mother of many" when I shared the hurt of losing my babies. I realized that prophecy when I became a teacher on the reservation. From the first day in the classroom, I recognized the look in the faces of those children. I could see through the masks, because for years I wore the same mask.

Many of us wear masks to hide our authentic selves. It's time to take off those masks. For many of us, that means rewriting our life story. I'm grateful I had an opportunity to rewrite my story. I no longer had to repeat the pattern of my mother and grandmother. I realized I could change the trajectory of my story. I understand hardship and the need for finding a safe place to make decisions. Like most of us, there's a natural gravitational pull to dysfunction.

I've created a tribe of authentic women who know the power of being authentic and true to who they are. This tribe of women understand that together, we are better. My passion is to help others live the best possible version of themselves. TRIBE is a community of like-minded women who support each other in their journeys to becoming their truest, most authentic selves. It's time to take off the mask that is holding you back. There is so much freedom in sharing your authenticity.

# Barbara Galutia Regis

**Author, Advocate and Physician Assistant**

*H*eart Word: Dream Big / Every time I am thrown challenges or "curve balls," I feel there's a much bigger purpose that I am experiencing and learning that can help others in a very huge way! That's what keeps me moving and believing!

Barb is a Family Practice Physician Assistant (PA) with a passion for education and advocacy. After graduating from AT Still-Kirksville College of Medicine founding class in 1997, she practiced at several Maricopa County primary care clinics serving the poor. Currently, she works for Premise Health at Insight Enterprises in Tempe, AZ as a solo practitioner and health center manager providing primary care to employees and families on campus. She was also a founding partner in Renaissance Medical Group and Renaissance Medical Properties with practices located in Chandler and Maricopa, AZ for 14 years. She had a dual role as Chief Operations Officer and practicing PA for 14 years. During her time at Renaissance, she was a PA preceptor and assisted with training 3rd-year medical students that rotated through their practice. Barb also served as an adjunct professor for the Northern Arizona University PA program.

Barb started Best of Health Advocacy and *Ask the PA* in 2013 with the goal of empowering patients and families to realize a better health care experience. She hosts Ask the PA on her *Best of Health* radio show and podcast on Phoenix Business Radio X. Along with being a PA, she is the author of the book Surviving the "Business" of Healthcare, Knowledge is Power!, a certified Medical Professional Legal Consultant, Patient Advocate, speaker, and a stage 3b melanoma survivor. Barb is also certified by the National Commission on Certification of Physician Assistants and is an active member of the American Academy of Physician Assistants.

# The Path Back Home

## By Barb Regis

My love of medicine started at an early age. I was fortunate to grow up in a loving home with parents that were so supportive of their community. My dad was the family doctor in a small Pennsylvania town called Coopersburg. My mom not only raised my two older brothers and me, but she supported my dad's practice as his bookkeeper/biller and greatest supporter. Office visits in those days were $9, and his office was located in our home. The concept of health insurance was just evolving, so it is fair to say he practiced medicine in a much simpler time—or was it?

My gut feeling is that in those days, there were a lot of bartering services for healthcare. My parents had a huge influence on my life as they truly were the ultimate givers and advocates.

My childhood, for the most part, was pretty normal, at least to me. As kids, we worked really hard. Each of us contributed to the household, whether it was yardwork, or weekly chores. In turn, we received opportunities to participate in activities that many others didn't, as my parents believed in experiences, not "things." For me, these experiences included my music, riding horses, and playing golf. Our neighbors helped teach me how to swing a golf club.

Considering my dad was a doctor and patients were coming to our home for care, it exposed me to many situations I would have never encountered. It was eye-opening for me. I was the kid in the corner listening and taking in all this information like a sponge. At that time, there was no Health Insurance Portability and Accountability Act (HIPAA), so I listened intently.

For a moment, imagine being "ground central" for all kinds of tragedies. In our home, we hosted families of loved ones as they waited to hear the status of their family member while my dad was the first responder at an apartment explosion down the street. There was a lot of coffee and dessert served to strangers and friends during those moments. In our kitchen, a family friend and coach for my brother admitted he was an arsonist. Little did I know then how much those interactions would influence who I was to become as an adult.

My parents encouraged my brothers and me to study hard while growing up and get a college education. We all took different directions in life. Dave, my oldest brother, got his degree in broadcasting and has been live on the air and managing radio stations ever since. My brother, Richard, holds degrees in safety management and hospital administration and has his own consulting company in Pennsylvania. I ended up going to multiple universities on a music scholarship as a euphonium player. Music was a path I needed to explore with a hope of landing a job performing in one of the premier military bands. I knew it was all or nothing. I determined if I did not make it to Washington, D.C. as a musician, then one day I would pursue medicine like my dad and the two generations before him.

In the 1980s, service band openings were rare. Even though I placed well in a couple of auditions, it still was not good enough. Being dual degreed in music performance and education, I ended up teaching band to students in grades five through eight in Phoenix. This was a great experience as we developed a very strong band program. During this time, I learned a lot through teaching and became even more passionate about helping others. My amazing students taught me a lot about myself, for which I am grateful. After teaching in the Madison School District for five years, I decided to pursue my passion for medicine. I didn't know exactly how I was going to get there, but I knew "if there is a will, there is a way."

In pursuit of this goal, I volunteered and finally worked as a Physical Therapy Tech (PT Tech) in the Maricopa County Hospital in Phoenix. I was exposed to critically ill patients and learned about medicine from physicians, nurses, and therapists. It was rewarding to help burn patients and amputees get healthier and stronger. These types of experiences confirmed I was on the right path.

While working in the burn center, I heard about Arizona's first physician assistant (PA) program through Kirksville College of Osteopathic Medicine. At that point, I was working towards medical school but after speaking with a couple of primary care PAs, I decided to apply to the program. In 1995, I was fortunate to get accepted into the first class.

Upon reflecting, I am one of just 26 students who were the first to graduate from a PA school in Arizona. Today, thousands have graduated as a PA because of the program. After graduating, I knew I would continue the family tradition of being a primary care provider just like my dad. I also knew that one day I would own my own practice.

After graduation, I went back to the county and practiced in their clinics as a family medicine provider. I had great mentors there and again, experiences that I will never forget. One, in particular, stands out. It was early morning, and two very young boys came in with severe asthma exacerbations. A chopper landed in the back lot and swooped the kids down to the County Hospital. Their asthma was life-threatening, so they were in the ICU for a few days. I worked with one of the boys, and another provider worked with the other. We kept giving them oxygen and breathing treatments. We took care of them until they were well enough to go home.

The next week, the kids came back for a follow-up appointment with their mother and older brother. When the older brother saw me, he hugged me and thanked me for saving his brother's life! The mother was crying and also very grateful. Then the older brother gave me a $2 bill. I did not want to accept it because I knew the family was struggling financially, but at the older brother's insistence, I did. That was in 2001. To this day, that bill is still in my wallet. It reminds me why I do what I do. That bill has also gotten me through some rough and challenging days throughout the years.

I can proudly say that I accomplished the goal of practice ownership with my medical doctor (MD) business partner in 2003. I learned so much about business, operations, and practiced certain principles that I still live by today. We developed programs for uninsured patients and also integrated counseling into the practices. For me, it was all about the patient experience and relationships. Many concepts that I focused on way back then are mainstream discussions today. The business side was the most challenging, and I am grateful for the experience and the lessons it taught me. I am happy that today our medical practice has a new brand and is thriving under my previous business partner.

In 23 years of practice, I can say no day is like another. There is nothing dull about family medicine because you never know what the next encounter may be like. I have been through many journeys with patients and their families. The hardest cases are always the children. The worst days are delivering bad news, such as a cancer diagnosis.

You learn as a provider that there is so much more than the practice of the day-to-day in the office. I found myself spending time advocating and advising patients to ask the right questions and to get answers as they sought out care outside the office. Trying to help people navigate through our healthcare system led me to finish writing my book: Surviving the Business of Healthcare—Knowledge is Power.

The year 2017 provided the beginning of some of the most challenging times of my life. My parents' health was becoming more fragile with hospitalizations, and it was inevitable that they were going to need some sort of living changes.

I had started a new job through Premise Health at Insight Enterprises in Tempe, Arizona. It continues to be the perfect fit for me as I am providing care at their on-site clinic with great support and teammates that are awesome. It's an opportunity to put my "best practices" in play, provide care, and advocate. I absolutely loved receiving this opportunity and still do. While taking on this new role, I am able to focus more on my patients and less on running a business.

I eventually landed exactly where I believe I am supposed to be. Social media has allowed me to stay in contact and occasionally advocate for my previous patients. Previous patients and families know I am here for each and every one of them if they choose to reach out.

I was blessed to have overall very good health. To manage my stress, I started running again. I was a long-distance runner, and I ran over ten half-marathons and participated in a couple of Ragnar Relay events over a six-year period in my late 40s and early 50s.

Then, on April 4th, 2018, my life changed forever. I was overdue for a dermatology appointment. I had a lesion on my face that I thought might be a squamous cell carcinoma and another very strange growth on my right arm that was changing. At my husband's insistence, I scheduled an appointment and had three biopsies. Even though the third lesion was strange looking, I honestly thought worse case it was a nodular basal cell carcinoma that is easily treatable. Less than two months before, I had a patient come into our clinic, and his lesion looked exactly like mine. His turned out to be nodular basal cell carcinoma which I suspected I had. I was wrong.

When the call came, I was told I had squamous cell carcinoma on my face. Then there was a big pause, and the voice said, "You have a rare form of melanoma, and it is serious." I remember sitting back outside during our lunch break with my team and trying to process what I just heard. I had diagnosed a few melanomas over the years, but this was so different.

My next thought was most of these patients died within a couple of years with this type of diagnosis. How was I going to tell my husband and elderly parents this news?

My emotions were all over the place, but the reality was I had to go back in the office and see patients as though everything was okay. My advocate mode set in, along with the help of my amazing dermatology PA, Beth. I saw my general surgeon and oncologist that week. These are providers I have referred patients to over the years. Now I was in their hands.

It was a whirlwind experience that led to surgery the following week. I have a very long scar on my right arm as a reminder every day. Along with removing the primary tumor, I had three lymph nodes excised. Unfortunately, the biopsies revealed two out of the three nodes were positive for cancer. This led me to being diagnosed with Stage 3b amelanotic melanoma. I go into detail about that entire journey in my book.

Melanoma is the most-deadly form of skin cancer, and it is tricky. This skin cancer can kill, and until this last decade, for many, it was a death sentence. My melanoma was not black or superficial; it was pink and nodular. It was rare, a fast grower that grows deep. That is why it is so dangerous and considered one of the deadliest forms of cutaneous melanoma. Had I been diagnosed just a year earlier, there would have been no other treatment other than waiting and a scan. In 2018, a new form of treatment called immunotherapy was approved for the treatment of Stage 3-4 metastatic melanoma. This therapy turbocharges the immune system to recognize and destroy cancer cells, specifically melanoma.

There are serious risks that I was willing to take because immunotherapy, in my opinion, was a gift, and the data concerning prolonging survival was showing that. The five-year survival rate increased with the therapy. Before therapy, my chance for recurrence was greater than 40 percent, and now it is less than 10 percent.

After 26 treatments with Opdivo (nivolumab), my last PET scan showed no evidence of cancer. I have some residual side effects, but I consider myself one of the lucky ones. I continue with my three-month skin evaluations and oncology appointments. Twelve biopsies later, so far so good. Avoiding the sun, keeping covered up, and using sunscreens are my norm. I am grateful to everyone on my team locally and especially to Dr. James Allison, the researcher at MD Anderson Houston who recently won the Nobel Peace Prize for his discovery of immunotherapy. There is a documentary available in many cities about him and his story. He is truly my hero and saving the lives of many melanoma and other types of cancer patients.

During my treatment journey, my family's lives unraveled. My parents could no longer stay in independent living. We moved them several times. Unfortunately, between the two of them, there were five hospitalizations, three rehabilitation stays, three different living facilities, and eventually my mom's death on October 24th, 2018.

Her untimely death could have been avoided. This experience has motivated me even more to advocate for tighter regulations for the safety of our elders. What is standard in the community today is not acceptable. It was exhausting and just so sad to observe what my mom went through physically and emotionally. Even though I tried to advocate for her, it was not good enough. I kept on asking myself, "Why me? Why now? What can possibly be the greater good from all this?" I promised my mom as she passed that her death would not go without change and accountability.

My book was published shortly after my mom's death, as there were a few short chapters that needed to be added from what she taught me. My dad has continued to adjust to his new home without mom. I am grateful to his amazing home health nurse, Cassie, who was there for both my mom and dad. She is another hero.

My husband's parents are both deceased. His mom was a nurse who died of pulmonary fibrosis. Her death was brutal, and there are so many unanswered questions about that horrible disease. His dad died suddenly at home of a heart attack. He was a victim of elder abuse and fraud; this was another reason I was compelled to write my book.

Through my journey and relationships, I have met a lot of people that need support and guidance. My brother-in-law was another example of someone with a family who owned his own business and had no health insurance. With research, he found physicians to perform surgeries at reasonable negotiated rates and medications from overseas at a fraction of the cost for a chronic illness. We would chat about ways to share and disseminate information he had researched. He was another tragic loss for our family as he died unexpectedly while flying in his private airplane in January 2019.

In February 2019, after 14.5 years of pure joy, Abby, our Old English Sheepdog, passed away. She was one of the greatest gifts a family could have. She was with me through all the tough days. She was so loved, and I am beyond thankful to her. My husband and I miss her every day.

The question "why" has continued to resonate with me as I believe things happen for a reason. Everything that has happened has led me in a different direction and motivated me to take action. Because of my mom's death and my interest in law, I am working as a Medical Professional Legal Consultant. I have received the trademark for Best of Health Advocacy and was honored by my colleagues as one of the Top 10 Physician Assistants in the country for 2019.

I am continuing to support and advocate for my friends, patients, fellow cancer warriors/families, and anyone that needs me. I have met some amazing people through my cancer journey from all over the world. They are now my friends and family. We help each other out and celebrate victories together.

Originally, as part of this book chapter, I hoped to share details concerning my legacy project. This project idea was the result of that moment where you say to yourself, "What is the reason for all of this?" There has to be a reason for all the pain, grief, and interactions with so many amazing people. I had that "aha" moment when I started thinking about a way to put all of my experiences, connections, and my passion for helping others into a project. But as quickly as it began to come together, it all started coming apart. Unfortunately, my project is on temporary hold due to pending litigation in Houston, Texas. I will not rest until I can move forward.

For now, my passion project is out of my hands, and I know that I will prevail. This has been one of my biggest disappointments and setbacks because now I have to rely on the legal system to allow me to move forward.

In the meantime, I choose to share my knowledge with others through my book, my website AskthePA.com, YouTube, Best of Health podcasts at Phoenix Business Radio X, and one encounter at a time.

Each day is a gift, and my journey has taught me a lot about gratitude, patience, and not taking anything or anyone for granted. I am so fortunate to have support from my husband, Tony, family, friends, colleagues, coworkers, and our new pooch, Jewlz.

In life, you have a choice of feeling sorry for yourself or taking these overwhelming challenges and learning from them and doing great things. To me, doing great things is the only option!

Here's to your Best of Health! Ask the PA

# Elena Porter

## Founder of I Am 360

*H*eart Word: Love Wins / Life is a journey of peaks and valleys. I once heard a quote, "You are in something, coming out of something, or about to go into something else. It is what we call life." There are very few guarantees in life except you will have a journey. But what I have learned is that God is good, Hope is real, Faith grounds you, Peace is possible, and Love always wins.

Elena Porter is the pioneer of Christ-centered yoga. In 2002, Elena created a unique version of yoga where she combined her Christian faith with the practice of yoga. At that time, if you searched for Christian yoga on the web, there was nothing to be found. She started this journey with just two students and over the past 17 years, the yoga ministry has grown to thousands of students. Elena's yoga practice inspires people at a soul level. She knows that for each life, each soul she impacts to see life differently, to gain new perspective, to see life through the lens of love, to give more, to accept others, to seek peace, that one lovingly impressed soul affects multiple other souls.

I AM 360 was created to represent all that Elena wants to be and influence others to be. I AM is a powerful statement of all that is true, good, and beautiful, and 360 is about being fully transformed and rooted in love.

Elena's dreams for I AM 360 are to be, and encourage others to be, the difference, to inspire people to want to be intentional with their words, actions, and choices and to pay attention to life and all that is going on around them.

Elena has taken her inspiration on the road. She is speaking to groups on Finding Your Happy, Practicing Your Purpose, Changing Your Story, Being the Difference, and Kindness Matters to encourage all people to live life with purpose, to spread love and light in this world.

# Find Your Feet

## By Elena Porter

I'm a southern California girl, born and raised. My family spent many weekends at the beach. As kids, we would play in the water with a Frisbee and build sand castles. My sister and I loved to go out in the ocean and get flung around by the waves until we didn't know what side was up. The bigger the waves, the better. Every now and then, a huge wave would get us. We would be tossed around and turned upside down. At times, we didn't know if we would make it out alive. During these moments, we were afraid we wouldn't survive. But, we knew all we needed to do was find our feet. If we could find our feet and root them into the sand, we could stand up no matter how powerful the waves were. This was a powerful life lesson. We learned that when life turns you upside down, find your feet, root down, and courageously rise up. That lesson is something I take to heart to this day.

**When life gets overwhelming, all you need to do is find your feet.**

I was the baby of the family until I wasn't. I was just shy of 7 when my twin brothers were born. Now we were a family of eight kids. My mom told me I would always be the baby of the girls. I knew she saw the nervousness in my eyes that I no longer was her baby. I was a momma's girl. Not only did I love her, I also admired her. I couldn't imagine living a day without her. My mom could always pick up on how people felt. I am grateful for the same gift. My mom told me I was born smiling and never stopped. I could always find the good in a situation, no matter how difficult. Throughout my life, friends would ask me to find the good news in a bad situation. I could always find a silver lining, a sliver of hope, no matter how remote or dismal the situation.

Our family loved music. There was always someone dancing, singing, or playing an instrument. Music and lyrics made my soul come alive. When I was sad, confused, or just a bit down, a good song could change the trajectory of my day.

I got married at 18 and had four kids back-to-back in 4 ½ years. My dream of being a high-powered attorney wearing pretty pink suits and working in the tallest building in Los Angeles was replaced with reality—babies, diapers, and amazing chaos. I never looked back. My husband and I went to computer technical school to become computer programmers. Our careers were launched, and time passed very fast. Maybe that was because it was Orange County, and everything seemed faster in California. Days turned into months, which then turned into years.

Our kids were growing, and it seemed like we were working more and more. We couldn't catch a break until we got the phone call with an opportunity to move to Arizona and start our own business. Without thinking too much about how it would be living in a new state and a new city where we had no family nearby, we packed up and moved. My parents promised to come visit often. My mom said, "Don't worry, baby girl, you are going to be so busy with your growing family. I will miss you more than you miss me."

At the time, I was not sure it was true about missing me more, but she was right. I was so busy raising kids and working, I had little time to think of anything else. Shortly thereafter, my mom and dad followed us to Phoenix, Arizona. Apparently, my mom was right about how much she would be missing me.

Our days were filled with sports, gymnastics, dance, and church activities. We felt blessed. Our business was doing well, and our family was healthy. Better yet, my parents lived in the same city as me, and seven of my eight siblings were now living in Arizona as well. Life was full. Then, something happened that would change our lives forever. I was pregnant again. It was over ten years since my fourth child was born. This new baby was nothing short of a miracle as my husband had an irreversible, permanent vasectomy. Life was about to get a little crazy, but our kids were thrilled. It felt like our little baby was about to inherit three moms and three dads. He brought much joy into our family. And a lot of work. I would soon have a toddler and four teenagers, and life got real very fast.

**It felt like there was a big wave crashing into me. I needed to find my feet.**

I found my feet, and we stepped into our new normal. I assured my youngest son prior to the baby's arrival that he, too, would always be my baby. I was trying to keep life balanced, but with four teenagers and a toddler, there was always something going on. For me, I realized the saying, "You are only as happy as your saddest child," was a reality for me. For the first time, I was having trouble finding peace and balance in my life. I needed something to calm my anxieties, when someone suggested yoga. I am a runner; I like to run up hills. Being still wasn't one of my strengths. But after three people suggested it, I decided to give it a try.

One hour of yoga provided a peace and calm I never knew before. That energy followed me home. Thinking it must have been a fluke, I went back the second day and had the same beautiful experience. My life was about to change in a good way. Practicing, reading, and studying yoga became my obsession. However, I never felt the spiritual experience that others claimed. A few months later, I had what I refer to as a God moment. I asked myself, "What if I put the focus and intention of my yoga practice on my faith?" I put together a playlist of random inspirational music, a Bible verse, and an inspirational quote. I marched out into my garage, which by the way, was about 110 degrees. I meditated, practiced yoga, and had a spiritual connection I have never felt before. I ran back into the house and told my husband. He chuckled and said, "Well, it is 110 degrees in that garage. Are you sure you aren't having a heatstroke?" I assured him that was not the case.

I knew something big had just happened. What I didn't know was in that moment, the first faith-based yoga practice was born. I started practicing my faith-based yoga every day in my hot garage. A couple weeks later, at church, Pastor Greg noted he was launching a sports ministry and wanted someone to lead a class. My husband nudged me and said, "Why don't you do what you do in the garage?" During the next 30 minutes of the sermon, I didn't hear a thing our pastor said. All I heard was an inner voice saying, "You know you are supposed to do this." Sigh. Sometimes when you do something new, there comes a sense of fear. I kept thinking, "What will people think of me? I'm not even a certified yoga instructor. Who am I to think that I could create something so new and innovative?"

As we entered the lobby, there was Pastor Greg. My mouth started to talk without my permission as I said, "Hi Greg, how about I start Christian Yoga here at the church? It's brand new, and no one has ever heard of it." I remember he did a head tilt and said, "What? Tell me again what it is." I blurted out, "It's Christ-Centered Yoga." There, I said it out loud.

Without any hesitation, Pastor Greg said, "Let's do it." He put it in the church bulletin, and the next Monday, I had my first class of three people. Christ-Centered Yoga was born. Pastor Greg was one of the participants. I was so happy. I honestly didn't think anyone would show up. The next week there was just one lady. For several months, she was my only student. Those months taught me a very valuable lesson. I learned the value of one soul. It didn't matter if one or 100 people showed up. If I could move, inspire, motivate, and love one soul, I knew the ripple effect would be expediential.

**Even in the good, sometimes you need to find your feet. Good can be scary, too.**

That one soul/person turned into hundreds, which have turned into thousands of people that have been touched through this yoga outreach. Of the participants, about 33 percent of the people go to my church, 33 percent don't go to any church, and 33 percent attend church elsewhere. No matter what their faith, people come to be inspired. They come to hear positive messages. They come to collectively and individually connect with God. They come just to feel love and be loved. We have grown to nine instructors who are there to share love and light and to make a difference.

In the meantime, life was full of raising kids and a baby, running a large outreach, and enjoying family, nature, and living healthy. We were absolutely enjoying life to the fullest and appreciating what we had. In 2006, however, our company closed down unexpectedly, and we found ourselves looking for jobs. It had been 20 years since we had to look for work, and the whole world had changed. Fortunately, before the recession grew worse, we found jobs.

In 2007, shortly after we started our new jobs, my dad became terminal with cancer. As I started to walk this very difficult road, I felt the heaviness and reality of when you know your time is limited with someone you love. I would care for my dad at night while my mom slept so she would have the strength to care for him during the day. Fortunately, I worked just a mile from their home. I, along with my siblings and my mom, were there when he took his last breath in April of 2008.

A few months later, my mom was diagnosed with cancer. At first, she looked like she was going to fight this battle, but after radiation, she fell into a deep depression. I spent months attempting to bring her emotional health back. She was sitting at my kitchen table when she proclaimed, "I will not fight this Elena, I am not your dad. I won't do chemo."

Reality was getting right in my face. Miraculously, a sense of peace came over me. I needed to just enjoy my mom for as long as she would be here. I had to respect her decision. She passed a couple of months later—11 months after my dad. As a self-proclaimed momma's girl, I was taken out of the game for a bit. A piece of me was gone.

This was a dark, unexpected time. We always said my mom was strong as an ox. We thought she would live forever. We didn't know that at the age of 75, she would pass, I believe, from the heartbreak of losing my dad.

**No matter how tragic the circumstance, I was always able to find my feet.**

When I lost my dad, I found my feet. I kind of had to. My mom needed me. When I lost my mom, I eventually found my feet. This took a little longer, but I did. My family needed me. And I found a way to muster the good news in all of this. The good news was she didn't die a cancer death. Her health failed her, and she died in the arms of one of her closest grandchildren, my son.

In 2010, my husband's health took a turn. We couldn't figure out what was happening. He started to have seizures, confusion, shaking, and headaches. He was diagnosed with chronic traumatic encephalopathy (CTE), a neurodegenerative disease caused by repeated head injuries. Mohammed Ali was diagnosed with CTE. My husband was a boxer, and most likely, that was the root cause. Nevertheless, he was abruptly disabled, and our income went from two to one. We had two kids in college, two in high school, and one in third grade.

**I knew what I needed to do; I needed to find my feet, and fast.**

It was hard, real hard. I was consumed with worry and anxiety about my husband's health, our finances, and the list goes on and on. But after many sleepless nights, fear, and tons of tears, I found my feet. We worked as a family to find our new normal.

Many times in my life, I needed to find my feet. Each time prepared me a little more to find them more quickly next time. I learned to trust my foundation of faith, anchor my feet firmly, and believe that I can stand up. I know I am not walking alone, and God will pick me up and set me on my feet when I need him to. I continued to be the one who could find the good news in any situation, just like when I was a kid. And then we were hit with an emotional tsunami. We lost our son.

**Game over. No finding my feet. Not this time.**

There were no words. I was in the biggest tsunami wave ever, and it was fiercely tossing me around and violently turning me upside down like I had never experienced before. I couldn't even remember how to find my feet. Life as I knew it would never ever be the same. And the odd emotion is you don't want it to be okay. Feeling pain is better than not feeling at all. I can't find words for what we went through in the first couple hours and days, but I do know with clarity that I heard my son's voice crystal clear. He said, "Mom, you are going to be okay." I was like, "No, I am not."

He said again with persistence, "But mom, you know you are." I again said out loud with a scream, "Not this time, I will never be okay." One more time, he said, "But you know you are." I paused and everything in me at the moment knew I was going to be okay, but I didn't want to be.

Year one was hell. There are no other words to describe it. I was in pain beyond anything I could comprehend. I got up and went to work. I was a zombie. I didn't speak much to anyone other than my husband, children, and sisters. I had a couple of friends who chose to walk the very dark road with me, and for that, I will be forever grateful. The first year was a blur. I tried my best to act normal for my kids and grandkids. We got together for all the firsts, and we cried a lot. No one grieves the same. Bless my beautiful children, they were hurting so bad, but they really tried to be there for my husband and me as we grieved differently.

It was the unsaid emotion that tore at my heart even more than the spoken emotion. I was a flipping wreck on the inside, as was my family. Besides work, I taught yoga, ran, hiked, and planned birthdays and holidays in a mechanical fashion. There's this saying about fake it till you make it, and I believe it to be true. I was a mess on the inside, deeper and darker than I cared to share with even myself. I received CDs to listen to from other women who have journeyed the same path as me. This was somewhat helpful. I listened to their stories and vowed to somehow do this grieving better, or at least differently than the other women.

Some of the women woke up five or ten years later and lost all those years. I vowed not to miss any memories with my children and grandchildren. Then year two came, and it was worse than year one. I didn't want to try anymore to "do it better" than others. I realized there isn't better. Life hurt; breathing hurt. There were moments when my heart hurt so bad I was sure it would stop beating. My children were hurting, too, as they missed their brother. My grandchildren were hurting because they missed their uncle. His beautiful daughter, who he called his little princess, a self-proclaimed daddy's girl, was crushed. We were about to enter a very dark time. For lack of a better word, we were screwed. But God had other plans.

My saving grace was this: my children and grandchildren brought me joy. Pain came with the joy initially, but when I was with them, there was more joy than pain in the moment. I learned to carry that with me when they left. I loved to talk about my son. I felt like if I talked about him, I was still around him. My family talks about him all the time. My family has grown even closer, if that was ever possible, because we need each other now more than ever. When one is struggling, there is another one of us to listen and hold each other's hearts. We all have our own way of grieving, and our love bond is deeper than ever.

One day, I was thinking about my son that passed and how he loved to wear positive message T-shirts. We shared a special connection with being positive and loving the world. When I had live music yoga events, he would arrive wearing the shirt I made for the event. Then, he started wearing them all the time. The T-shirts and those sayings were a piece of my life that my son and I shared deeply. We both had a love for music and how lyrics could move our souls. He would provide me with new yoga themes and playlists. One day he called me to ask, "Have you ever heard of the song 'Tell Your Heart to Beat Again'? It's about times in life when you are hit with great tragedy, and God sends you all the help in the world to heal you and help you to get better. He does this in a variety of ways, including people, songs, and books. There comes a time when you have to tell your heart to beat again." I feel like those words were his last gift to me. That was the last song he gave me. And years later, I realized he was right. I had to find my feet, take the help God sent, and tell my heart to beat again.

I now look at life through a different lens because of the loss of my son. As I began to look through this lens, the idea of I AM 360 came to me. I AM is a powerful statement of everything you want to be, 360 is about coming full circle in who you are designed to be, to become complete in who you are. Through I AM 360, I can carry on what we shared and encourage others to do the same.

I realized I felt the most healing when I was serving others, teaching yoga, and meditation, or participating in some outreach event. By facilitating a connection with God for my students, I felt hopeful. When I serve others, I feel like a little piece of my heart and soul begins to heal. I can create positive messages like my son used to wear. And just like my son, people can share these messages with the world. When they wear them, read them, and breathe in the message, something inside changes. I wanted to form a company where the profits of the shirts went to helping other people doing amazing, positive things in the world. How full circle would that be? I wanted to create a space where people could come together and serve others—those who are lonely, hurting, bored, or restless. As people come together while helping others, they begin to heal, grow, learn, and become.

I still hurt every day. I don't think an hour goes by that I do not have a memory, thought, or emotion of my son come to mind and my heart. Some days stink. Some moments my heart hurts so bad, I honestly think it could just stop. But then I pause and choose joy. I ask God to please use me. Sometimes it is in the smallest ways, and my heart feels joy, love, and a sense of peace. Sometimes it is in big ways, and I feel like he just parted the Red Sea for me to step into an experience and be love for someone.

When I speak and share my story, I ask people to pay attention to those in their circle and feel their needs. I often hear people say they do not know anybody in need. My answer is always, "Let's draw a bigger circle around you. If you still don't know anyone in need, I have some you can borrow." I have learned you don't have to be healed to be used, that joy is a choice. Finding my feet through all of this was a challenge, but I did it. The only real way you can heal your heart and soul is to serve others. Peace is possible. Love will win. Through I AM 360, I've created a positive message movement that provides opportunities to serve others and find true healing and peace.

Friends, I have found my feet. There are days still that I don't want to, but I hear that ever so sweet voice of my son saying, "But mom, you know you are going to be okay." You are right, son, God wins.

# Kristine M. Binder

**Educator, Coach, Ambassador, Advocate, and Fundraiser**

*H*eart Word: Forward / #forwardisapace is my motto, in running and in life. Giant leaps of baby steps, the #tutulady is always moving forward, leaving a little sparkle wherever she goes! Head up/wings out/tutu on ... Look forward/Move forward/Sparkle!

Best known as the #tutulady, Kristine is an elementary school teacher and Girls on the Run coach/site coordinator. As both an award-winning, veteran classroom teacher and coach, Kristine knows how to make connections and emphasize the strengths of her students and others. Kristine has faced the challenges of abuse, anxiety, depression, and divorce courageously and with determination. "Forward is a Pace" is Kristine's motto in running and in life. It has served her well, motivating her even in her darkest days. As when crossing the finish line in the many marathons she has run, she continually moves forward with a positive attitude through the many twists and turns of her life's journey, inspiring and empowering others along the way. Kristine is a firm believer in the powers of kindness, optimism, moving forward, and supporting others.

In addition to teaching and coaching, Kristine is a business woman and fashion stylist. As an entrepreneurial ambassador for a fair trade fashion brand, she is creating meaningful opportunities and employment for artisans in vulnerable communities throughout the world.

Kristine is an active volunteer as well as a strong vocal advocate for women's empowerment, mental health support, and an ally for the LGBTQ community.

Kristine is a single mother to five amazing, almost grown children. She is also a rescue mom to her sanity saver, Lucky. Kristine also enjoys yoga, cooking, knitting, reading and, like any good Chicagoan, is an avid Cubs, Hawks, and Bears fan.

You can always find her in her tutu, challenging others to relentlessly pursue their immeasurable potential.

# In Tutu Spirit and the Tutulady

## By Kristine Binder

I never planned to be a runner. I never liked working out or running, or anything fitness-related. I liked my watch what I eat and look at those crazy gym/running people lifestyle. I was never an athlete. An athletic supporter? Yes, I am a huge fan of football and hockey! But, actually being physically active? No thank you.

It took adopting an energetic dog, Wrigley, that required exercise, to get me moving. My motivation for running had nothing to do with me. It was about being more efficient. I thought jogging a lap around the park instead of walking would be faster and wear Wrigley out sooner. It turns out, it wore me out faster, not Wrigley! One day, in passing, I mentioned my running to a friend who dared me to run a local 5K (3.2 miles). I did it. That was over 14 years ago.

Running has never come naturally to me. I was the big-boned girl that was bullied in school and was picked last for everything. I have never been fast, and I have never won a race. Those ads for running gear with the woman effortlessly running for miles never seeming to break a nail or a sweat? Nope. Not me!

I am an endurance athlete. I run like a turtle in a vat of peanut butter—slower than molasses going uphill in a snowstorm. I am also not very coordinated. From day one, I just put one foot in front of the other and continued moving forward.

As I became more confident as a runner, I signed up for a WonderGirl race. Although I ran by myself, I felt at home during the race. The girl power was amazing, and the support phenomenal. At the time, I didn't know it, but this was what I had been looking and longing for all my life. The trajectory of my entire life would be forever altered. I know it sounds oh so dramatic, but truth be told, it really did change my life.

I later learned that the WonderGirl race was sponsored by Girls on the Run and was a culminating activity for the program. After many phone calls and some internet digging, I was courageous enough to start a program at my school. I discovered that Girls on the Run is a nonprofit program for girls ages 8-11. The program inspires girls to be joyful, healthy, and confident using a fun, experience-based curriculum which creatively integrates running. It took two years and an uphill battle to bring the program to my school. At the time, the program was relatively new and relatively unknown in our area. So, I had to fully vet the program and its sponsors for my school and the Archdiocese. My youngest daughter was in third grade when I finally started coaching the program at my school. My daughter and her friends would be my first team as a coach! Crossing the finish line with that team, and especially my own little girl, filled my heart with so much love and pride, I thought it might explode! It was a feeling of such accomplishment for all of us!

I continued running and training alone. I liked the time by myself to run and clear my head. I was also really intimidated by other runners. I was afraid that people would figure out how slow I was. I ran before the sun came up so I could be home when my kids got up, I ran on the treadmill so I could be home for my kids, and I ran around the park while my kids played. I just ran.

In 2009, I took a big leap and registered to run the Chicago Marathon to raise money for Girls on the Run. I trained alone that first year, reading everything about marathon training I could find, and asking questions in online chat rooms (yup, I am chatroom old!). Training for that first marathon was so difficult. During the race, I taxed my body because I just didn't know any better but to cross the finish line. That was one of the best feelings I have ever had in my life!

I decided to run the marathon again the following year, but this time I joined a training group to better prepare myself. It was the best decision I ever made. Running with others who ran my pace and the added accountability of weekly group runs helped me finally feel like a real runner. I was no longer alone. Today, my closest and dearest friends are from this group. They are like a second family to me.

Every Saturday, during our marathon training, we'd meet and head out for long runs. When running endless miles, talking fills the void. Runners talk about anything and everything on a long run. It is like moving therapy. Nothing is off-limits, and all guards come down. TMI (too much information) does not exist with runners! The long group runs with your BRF (best running friends) are a lot like Las Vegas—whatever is spoken on a long run, stays there. My group leader that year was exactly who I needed in my life. We cemented our friendship into family on those runs.

While training for the marathon, I coached my Girls on the Run team lessons of positive self-esteem and positive body image. What I didn't truly realize until much later was that I was the one that needed those messages. I needed to hear what I was teaching those girls. I was giving those girls what I wished I had been given growing up. While talking about negative self-talk during coaching, one of the girls said she didn't think, no, she knew, she could not finish the upcoming race. The team rallied around her to encourage her and then dared me to run my next race in a tutu if all the girls crossed the finish line. They all finished the race, which meant I had to keep up my end of the deal.

How did it feel wearing a tutu for the first time in a race? Holy cow! Tutu Spirit is real! I felt like I was flying through that race. I wanted every girl and woman to have that feeling. Tutu Spirit is the embodiment of the spirit of every girl on the run—past, present, and future. It is all of their positive energy, joy, silliness, struggles, faith, confidence, fortitude, power, strength, sparkle, and all the other wonderful, unique qualities that make up each girl. I felt so powerful that day wearing my tutu. As a result, I vowed that from that point forward, I would run every race in a tutu. Thus, the #tutulady was born.

Meanwhile, I was keeping a big secret. I was not happy. I looked happy and acted the part, but I was far from it. I was troubled. I was busy and had a full life, but happy? No.

I felt most like myself when I was running. It became a time when I was not in competition with anyone—a time when the voices in my head quieted down. I adopted the motto of forward is a pace, tagging every photo and blog post with that motto and the #tutulady hashtag. Looking back now, I realize that motto and the lessons of marathon training eventually saved my life.

I befriended some women runners online through internet chat rooms. We called ourselves Moms on the Run. We talked online daily and even met to run a few races together. I was stepping out of my comfort zone, expanding my circle, and making more friends.

I became more involved in Girls on the Run, worked full-time, ran with my running group, and managed my household. Meanwhile, my husband was working nights, so the heavy lifting of parenting was on me. The nights he was not working were special as the whole family was expected to be home for dinner. I loved those dinners with everyone around the table, laughing and joking. However, I began to realize that some of the jokes were not really funny, and feelings were getting hurt. Dinners often ended with someone leaving the table crying. I chalked it up to sibling rivalry and normal teen angst, but it was so much more. The stress level escalated when dad was home as everyone wanted his attention. The kids started picking up on his underhanded comments about me, and began attacking each other as well.

The barbs became more frequent. Nothing I did was good enough for my husband, and the kids followed his lead. My running, and especially the tutu, had become an additional source of embarrassment for my husband. He made sure I knew about it both in private and in public.

As the comments became more pointed and the arguments more frequent, the tension increased, and along with it came increased hostility. I felt like a stranger in my own home, more like the hired help than a mother and a wife. I struggled every day to keep the peace and keep everyone, especially my husband, happy. My stress levels shot through the roof as my anxiety and depression grew. I was slowly coming undone. So I kept running.

I did not talk about my feelings with anyone, not even my running group. I retreated into myself, becoming isolated and alone. I did not complain about my home life. I got dressed every morning, slapped on a smile and a positive attitude like it was a part of my outfit, and went about my day. No one knew the stress, anxiety, and depression that I felt, and if they did know, no one said anything. So I kept running, hoping to fill the void, healing my endless anxiety, and finding an end to the bottomless depression.

Running became my therapy of choice. I also knew it was not enough. So, I put my pride aside and secretly made an appointment with an actual therapist. She told me my anxiety and depression were due to my marriage. I laughed. I eventually stopped going to see her altogether. I was terrified she would see through me.

How could I tell her what was really going on? How could I let her in on my feelings of worthlessness and betrayal? How could I be open and honest? How could I leave a marriage of over 20 years when my husband kept telling me that no one would want a mother of five and I would end up alone? My therapist was not the one that had to go home and live in my house. I was. I was not only scared, I was also in denial. Therapy was not going to help me.

The distance between my husband and I increased. His emotional abuse grew worse as I found validation and acceptance outside my home through running and coaching. I was becoming more independent—something that was frowned upon and vilified by him. I kept teaching the lessons of positive self-esteem and body image to my Girls on the Run team, but I had yet to internalize them. It wasn't until I met the founder of Girls on the Run and got to personally thank her for what the program had given my daughter and other girls that I realized all those lessons I taught each season were for me to learn. So I began to internalize those lessons.

Meanwhile, I stuck it out in my marriage. Leaving a troubled marriage is never that simple. Women in physically, mentally, emotionally, or financially abusive relationships become conditioned to accept the abuse. Emotional, financial, and mental abuse is insidious. These types of abuse creep in and take over, especially because no one can see them coming, and there are no real visible or physical signs. The comments, putdowns, patronizing, blame, embarrassment, isolation, secrets, lies, name-calling, unpredictability, financial control, and dehumanizing take place slowly over time. Often, these signs don't raise alarm bells, and the victims don't realize this is really abuse. I know I did not. So I stayed.

I didn't know I was in an abusive relationship. I knew my husband was not nice to me, but I made excuses for him and blamed it on the stress of his job. After all, he did take me out once in a while, and he paid the bills (or so I thought). I was terrified that he would take my children away from me because he threatened to do it all the time. My kids have always been my kryptonite. I could not live without them and didn't want them to come from a broken home.

I was so ashamed. I kept blaming myself and thought if I changed my behavior, it would get better. The red flags were waving in all shapes and sizes, and I was just looking the other way. So I stayed.

After a few really horrible arguments, my daughters discovered their father had been unfaithful. Knowing my kids were aware of this, I could no longer condone his behavior. I mustered courage from a place I never knew existed and said, "Enough!" I had lived in fear long enough. Even though I was still terrified, I knew I deserved better—for myself and for my children. I decided to demand respect, stability, and fidelity from my husband. But, he decided to provide me with none of those things. I needed peace. So, I made the most frightening and difficult decision of my life and filed for divorce.

What followed were some of the most painful, messy, difficult, and expensive years of my life. Divorcing an abusive narcissist is no day at the beach. Okay, maybe, if that beach is in hell and you have a horrible sunburn. I made a ton of mistakes. I drank, I cried, and I just fell apart. I became a shell of myself. I lost myself and, in the process, almost lost my children. I was not the mother my children needed or deserved, but I was doing the best I could with what I had. And one of the things I had was running shoes. So I ran.

At a certain point, I could no longer hold myself together, so I let my running group and a few friends know about the shit show that was my current reality. I was afraid they would judge or avoid me because I was no longer full of sunshine, rainbows, and encouragement, but just the opposite happened.

What they gave me was unconditional love. The group became my safe harbor. They called me, they checked in on me, and when I did not show up for a run or did not answer, they came looking for me. They held me accountable, dragging me kicking and screaming sometimes, out the door. And we ran together. They would often ask me what I needed from a run. When I could not find the words, we would run in silence. Other times I would cry, scream, or emotionally vomit all over them while putting one foot in front of the other. No matter how difficult or unbearable I had become, they still showed up for me. I no longer felt alone because I wasn't. So I continued to run.

I returned to therapy, this time with a different therapist. Together we began to untangle the web of lies and unwrap the person I had hidden away. The verbal reel of negative and patronizing comments, put-downs, insults, and insecurity played over and over until I learned to reframe it and play a different tape. It took a lot of work, but I learned that bruises heal and fade away. Once I started to open up about my life and become more transparent, I realized I was not alone on so many levels. So many women were going through similar challenges, and dealing with issues that were unspoken or avoided altogether due to fear. So I kept talking, listening, and running.

I began owning my life and my choices. Owning my mistakes, messy parts, and fears took courage, but I offered myself the grace and forgiveness that I had so plentifully given to others for years. I was reclaiming myself and my life, and I was stronger than I gave myself credit for. I had survived losing almost everything and having been broken a million times over. Somehow, I was picking myself up and putting myself back together, stronger than before. By sharing my story with those that cared enough to listen, I was no longer a victim or a survivor. I was a thriver. I was becoming a true badass and a force to be reckoned with. I was that inspirational #tutulady!

I have always been cautious about sharing my story out of respect for the feelings of my children. Finding the silver lining and living with a positive outlook has been challenging. Some days are easier than others! But, I promised myself and my kids that I would always tell my story from a place of peace and respect. My children have suffered enough from the mistakes I have made, from the divorce, and the fallout from the divorce. I strive to set a better and more positive example for them.

My children now know that without question, I will always put them first, I will fight for them, and my love for them is unconditional no matter how old they are. My kids and I continue to work through boundaries and the difficult parts of life. Is it easy? Heck no! We are all a work in progress. My relationships with each of my five children are as individual and different as each one of them. However, none of those relationships would have been possible had I stayed in my marriage.

I do not believe in coincidences. I call them God Incidences. These are times where, if I look hard enough, I can see the hand and face of God. I have had many of these moments and can now see them for what they are. For years I had been surrounding myself with strong women who, not only led by example, but helped me find my own strength. I know that God has a plan. I may not always like it or understand it, but I have to trust it because some days faith is all I have left.

Through it all, running has remained my go-to, my safe space. When I feel lost or like I am losing my way, running reminds me I can always run home because my feet always know the way back. When I feel like I can't outrun the Negative Nelly voices in my head, running reminds me that I am an endurance athlete. Running offers me the grace that if I fail, I can always try again.

Running is also a constant reminder that change comes from challenges. Some runs are difficult (okay, some runs just suck) but running reminds me that I can do difficult things. Every season, my Girls on the Run are a reminder for me to dance, sing, and be silly. They remind me to always embrace the unexpected and that I still need to hear those lessons again and again.

Some runs, like real life, do not go as planned. However, running reminds me that I can lean in and keep moving forward. For the past 14 years, I have met some of the best people I know through running. It has given me experiences, taught me things about myself and others, and allowed me to see things I would have never seen. Running has brought me freedom.

When I first began running solo, I was truly running away from my circumstances. It was my attempt to run away from myself, anxiety, depression, cruelty, and abuse. It was exhausting. Today, I am clearly running towards something. Owning and sharing my story has allowed me the freedom to run towards myself, my life and my truth, inspiring others along the way. It is liberating!

As I share my journey, some people are inspired by honesty and vulnerability. Others don't relate because it does not include them or their story. I am ok with that. This is my story. This is me, and I am who I am. Take me or leave me. I have been told that my personality can fill a room. I am okay with that. I am done denying and apologizing for who I am. I am done with being shamed into silence. I have been given a chance to live life on my terms, and I will not waste it.

We women have been sold a bill of goods that we need to be a size zero, always be happy, find a man that can take care of us, marry by the time we are 30, have kids, remain quiet, and stay in our place. You know what? None of it matters if you are not being true to yourself. None of it matters if you do not love yourself and who you are. None of it matters if you are being treated as less than. No matter what your size, feel comfortable in your own skin. Stand up for yourself and those that you love.

None of us are better than anybody else. We all have fears and insecurities, and we all feel less than perfect from time to time. When one of us succeeds, it does not diminish others. That is so far from the truth. We need to embrace and celebrate what makes us unique and different. We need to support and lift each other up. We need to open doors for others to own their own story. Women are powerful when we believe in ourselves and in each other, and we are unstoppable when we channel our energy towards a positive purpose.

The WonderGirl race inspired me to keep moving forward and get involved. Girls on the Run taught me to love myself and to find my inner strength. I wear a tutu at each race for one reason—to share the Tutu Spirit with everyone. We all deserve the feelings of confidence, strength, and joy that come from fully owning who we are.

Being the #tutulady allows me to leave a little sparkle wherever I go, and to represent all that is possible once you are courageous enough to embrace yourself—flaws, insecurities, and all. You don't need to wear a tutu to catch the contagious #tutuspirit, but as the #tutulady, I hope I can inspire you to always move forward, find your own #tutuspirit, and let your inner #tutulady shine!

# *Dr. Kristy Morgan*

**Arizona Director of Candle Wishes Foundation Arizona/
Vice President and COO of Unity Physician Services**

*H*eart Word: Be the Change / Today I bought the person in line behind me at Chick-fil-A for their meal. My son asked me why. I said, "I usually always do it when I am at Starbucks, but never an entire meal." The girl who took my order said, "It's my pleasure to serve you." My son asked if I have ever been the recipient of someone buying my drink or a meal. Honestly, I haven't, and I told him it really didn't matter because if my act of kindness started a chain behind me, that's all I needed.

Dr. Kristy Morgan has been the owner and operator of Pain Stop Avondale, a multi-disciplinary chiropractic and medical office in the West Valley, for the past 10 years. She is also currently the Vice President/Founding Member of Unity Physician Services, a management company that helps other physicians create an integrated health and wellness model for their patients. Her most current passion, however, is her newest endeavor as the Arizona Director of a 501c3, Candle Wishes. Candle Wishes is a nonprofit that enriches the lives of underprivileged and homeless children in the community through the celebration of their birthdays with gifts and birthday parties that they may not otherwise receive. It is through Candle Wishes that Dr. Morgan is able to pursue a lifelong desire to serve others in the community.

With her vast entrepreneurial skills, she is also able to help fulfill a dream for the founder of Candle Wishes to help it grow to other communities throughout the country. The goals of the foundation are to be a nationwide household name by 2020 and Dr. Morgan is the one that will make that happen!

# Finding My Purpose by Finding My Voice

## By Dr. Kristy Morgan

All my life, I have been looking for my voice. Even as a little girl, I struggled to find it. I am, what you would call, an introverted extrovert. If I knew you back then, I was all in on our friendship. If you were new to me, I was extremely shy to the point that I would make myself sick worrying about what you thought about me. I didn't feel comfortable sticking up for myself. As a result, I would back down from situations even if I knew I deserved better. My self-confidence and self-esteem suffered, too. To add fuel to the fire, I had extreme anxiety, which didn't allow me to take advantage of opportunities or try new things outside of what I was comfortable with.

As a kid, my anxiety came with bouts of mild depression. At that time, I had no idea what anxiety and depression really meant, how it affected my body, and how to control it. My parents didn't understand it either. My anxiety gave me flu-like symptoms that manifested itself throughout my body. My stomach, joints, and hands hurt. To deal with the symptoms, I'd simply stay away from social situations that I was not comfortable in. My lifestyle was more avoidance than social. I was always up for trying new things, but many times I did not do that because it meant that I had to put myself out there. I was not comfortable having new experiences.

Growing up, I lived in a wonderful home with very loving parents in Canada. Our entire family pretty much lived within a few miles of each other. Most of my relatives worked in a family business or were entrepreneurs of some sort. I grew up surrounded by lots of aunts, uncles, and cousins, but I kept to myself as much as

I could. I was desperately trying to find my voice back then, but the anxiety kept me from reaching out. My family considered me to be a happy, popular, outgoing girl who had lots of friends. That wasn't necessarily untrue. I guess I was all of these things at different times in my life, but never all at once. I constantly compared myself to my outgoing, not shy cousins, who seemed to have wonderful lives. I wanted that for myself someday. They appeared to have found their voices early on.

I lived in my hometown all of my life. After graduating from high school, it was time to leave to attend college. At this point, my anxiety was so out of control that instead of moving further away and going to the school where I really wanted to be, I stayed close by. While I loved the excitement of finally living on my own, I just could not jump into something so new, so far away. Even if it was only two hours away from home, I couldn't do it. To say I regretted this decision for a very long time is quite true. However, looking back, I would have never been on the path that I am currently on. I now understand the true meaning of "everything happens for a reason." Despite being so homesick for my small town and what I perceived as normal, I truly wanted so much more but had no clue how to get it.

During my college years, I was in a very toxic relationship (if you could call it that), which I finally realized was completely my fault. Even though I knew this relationship was not healthy, somehow, the toxicity felt comfortable. It was like a bad habit I couldn't shake. Despite the person not wanting to be with me, I developed this mindset that he was the one I was destined to be with, and, this is how life was supposed to be. I didn't know any better, and felt being close to home was my only choice. At some point, I would need to eventually settle down and get a job. That's what all grown-ups do, right? I was so uncomfortable with my current life, and extremely uncertain and scared about the future and where

I fit in. So, I kept going back to what was familiar because the thought of change terrified me. I did not have the skills to properly address this issue. I was young, naïve, and just wanted to be loved no matter what.

Then something hit me like a ton of bricks. I finally saw a glimpse of what my life would continue to be if I stayed on the track I was on. It was not pretty. I needed out. I needed to get away for my own sanity. I was at a breaking point mentally. I am so proud of myself for being able to finally recognize this pattern of self-destruction and commit myself to finding a better path.

Nobody expected me to go far away to graduate school, let alone go to a school in another country, but I did. Although I didn't have my voice yet, I was desperately searching for it. So, I packed up my car on Mother's Day weekend (my mother will never forgive me for this) and took a ten-hour drive to St. Louis, Missouri. In the rearview mirror were everything I've ever known—my family and friends. But, I knew in my heart, it was time to start a new life. I didn't know what that would look like, but I knew it would be nothing like the life I just left.

For the first time ever, I made a decision and just went with it. I was learning what it was like to find my voice. And it felt good.

My people-pleasing days were over with, and I was excited to add the title "Doctor" to my resume. By cramming over five years of school into about three and a half years—I graduated with my doctorate with a new life in front of me. The group of students I went through school with became my extended family during this time. I met my future husband during graduate school and created lifelong friendships with others that are now my business partners.

An entrepreneur at heart, I took my career in chiropractic and led with that entrepreneurial spirit so infamous in my family. At first, my husband and I each started our own chiropractic offices.

As someone who was extremely independent, even though we were both chiropractors, I didn't feel the need to go into business with him. We started our own companies in two different towns about 20 minutes apart out in Pennsylvania. Even though I was still struggling to find my voice, I didn't want to be swallowed up into the concept that I was his wife and was simply there to serve in a support role. I worked just as hard to get my degree as he did, so I always wanted to feel like we were equal. For about five and a half years, we built our businesses before relocating to Phoenix.

Finding my voice has been an ongoing journey. There was a time about 13 years ago, where I tried to assert myself, and I was not properly educated on the situation. I was part of a small group that were interested in an agenda that I was not fully aware of. I wanted to "fit in" and feel like I had some meaning in my life; however, I was too quick to speak without fully knowing the entire situation. As I look back on it, I can now see how my actions were wrong. I used my voice for someone else, not myself, and truly regret how the scenario unfolded. I wish I would have handled it better. It is one of those situations where maybe only one or two people may remember, but it will stay with me forever because I wasn't speaking for myself.

More recently, I am learning how to structure using my voice in my own company as I am one of seven owners AND the only female. I have always been very straightforward with my staff on how I wanted things done. As our company has grown, I've discovered that it's important to tailor my tone and presentation based on who I am talking to in order to get my point across effectively.

Until recently, I was unfamiliar with personality assessments. As a business owner, I felt it was my way or the highway. I quickly learned that not everyone thought the way I did or dealt with situations the same way I did. If I wanted to grow as a business owner and a person, I really needed to be able to interact with my staff in a way that allowed both them and the business to grow. It was a tough scenario, not getting my way all the time, but by learning how others react to situations because of their personality style, I began tailoring my questions and answers to their personality. As a result, our company has benefited from better communication. We use the DISC assessment tools in our business. I have never had any formal training in personality assessments, so over the years I have learned the hard way that there actually is a better way to get your point across without alienating individuals.

The DISC tool allowed me to better understand how other people might react to a situation. For example, one of my employees needs time to assess a situation before jumping in and making any changes. I, on the other hand, know what I want and just do it. If I need them to help me, I present my idea to them in a way that they can absorb and then give them time to marinate on the process before coming back with an implementation solution. If I didn't give them the proper time that they needed, more likely than not the process would have been jumbled, unorganized, and chaotic. Some people just can't handle abrupt change. They need time to process the entire situation before coming to a solution. If a little bit of extra time saves us undue stress in the long run, I needed to change my ways! Finding my voice was/is a constant learning process for me, so why should I have thought it was any different for anyone else?

After years of hard work, I realized one day that I was not asserting my voice loud enough.

One afternoon, our group of friends was hanging out. We had all known each other for a very long time. However, there were some new people who had only been in our lives for a few years. When I noted I was one of the owners of the practice, one of our newer friends looked at me and said, "You own the company with these other guys? I thought you were just their secretary."

I responded, "Are you kidding me?" He replied, "Kristy, I really thought you were married to Tom and just ended up as his secretary." That was an eye-opener for me. It was something that we joke about to this day, but deep down, after all these years of trying to assert my independence from my husband, who holds the same degree as me, it seemed that I had failed.

That's when I realized that I needed to step it up.

I was that one girl, and they automatically assumed I was the secretary.

Then something happened that woke me up in a way I never expected. I couldn't move my arms. I thought I was having a seizure. Because I couldn't move my arms, I thought I was paralyzed. I was at work when it happened. I thought I'd sit down for just a minute and it would go away. I was lucky I wasn't driving, as I was ready to leave. At work, there were people there to help. I went to the hospital where I was misdiagnosed with having a seizure. Because I was so young, at age 35, they never suspected I was having a stroke. Because they thought I was having a seizure, I was soon released from the hospital. The next day I was still dizzy, so my husband took me in for an MRI. The MRI scan revealed something none of us expected—I was having ministrokes.

I was in the hospital for four days. They did every type of test imaginable. One of the very last tests was the bubble test to check for holes in the heart. Guess what? I had a hole in my heart. The clot went through a small hole in my heart and up the wrong artery. All these years of playing sports and having a child, no one had ever caught this defect. As a result, for the next three years, I was on blood thinners because of my risk factor. Eventually, I had the hole in my heart repaired with a small device that sealed up the area.

Here's the thing—having a near-death experience wasn't the changing point in my life. The real light bulb went off when I realized my kids were getting older and didn't need me like they did when they were little. That was the true wake-up call. I was nearing 40, starting to feel my mortality, not yet empty nesters, but had teenage kids who didn't rely on me as much. Here I am, a somewhat healthy, energetic person who set out on a path to change her life for the better, accomplished so many milestones in life and business over the years, but I still felt empty. That was when I realized that finding my voice only got me so far. I was missing my true passion in life. I was finally coming full circle. I was finally seeing that God created me to be kind and caring and have a heart and love deeply for a specific reason. What I thought was always my character flaw was actually my true calling, hidden beneath layers of anxiety and not knowing how to assert myself appropriately (with my voice). Forty years later, I am finally realizing that my desire to help people was not "being the nice Canadian," it was not a character flaw, it is just me. It's who I am and who I was meant to be. I finally understand how finding my voice was my stepping stone to finding my passion. This intense understanding that my purpose and destiny in life was not yet completed led me to find an amazing foundation, Candle Wishes, that I now run in Arizona.

Candle Wishes is a faith-based 501c3 that serves underprivileged and homeless children in our community with birthday parties and gifts. The Arizona chapter has been in operation just over a year now and will have thrown seven parties by the end of 2019. This gives 280 children gifts, love, hope, and memories they may not have received or experienced otherwise on their birthday. Not only do we serve the children, we also invite families to celebrate and have fed over 840 people at these parties. Seeing the impact we are starting to make on our Arizona communities has me thinking it's time to make that impact even bigger!

The moral of the story is that life can change unexpectedly. One day you are living in a small town in Canada, and the next day, you are running a company in the fifth-largest city in the US. If I had let my fear and anxiety dictate my life, I would not have had all the wonderful experiences that have led me to be able to share my story with others who may be feeling the same fear and anxiety I had when I was young. I began realizing that the way we start thinking about ourselves is how people start treating us. When you find your voice, you start getting treated like you deserve to be treated.

How are you showing up in life? When you sit back and take a hard look, is that the reason why you are being treated a certain way?

I wish there was somebody to mentor me when I was a shy, awkward girl trying to navigate the system, but when the world seems so small, it's hard to see outside of it. I want to share the message that there is a world out there that is ready to be discovered. It doesn't matter what your obstacle is; it is there waiting for you. Never give up. Better yet, if you want to make an impact on the world, go find your voice. By doing so, it will help you achieve so much more. Go after it. You won't regret it.

# Lynn Brown

**Author**

*H*eart Word: Faith / When all is done, and my day is finished, I shall look back at my life and see the triumphs and struggles. The triumphs were fun. The struggles were a special gift. They strengthened my Faith, showing that I was never left to do battle alone. Life will never be perfect and will always have its ups and downs. But with Faith, I can weather the storm in a safe harbor. I only pray, on my final day, to hear the words spoken in Matthew 25:23: "Well done, good and faithful servant."

Lynn Brown lives in Kirkland, Washington with her husband Greg. After two wonderful careers in retail buying and sales, she decided to retire and enjoy every moment of her young family's life. This allowed Lynn to volunteer as room mom, team mom, and chaperone for as long as their children, Max and Anna, would let her. Lynn is also a church volunteer, gardener, and caretaker of their cottage, as well as the author of her novel Three.

# A Mom's Christmas

## By Lynn Brown

"I knew you'd find a way to get me up there for Christmas!" Mom laughed. I could just see her shaking her head at the other end of the phone. Mom and I spoke every day if only to say, "Hi", or glean a bit of advice on any new wrinkles that may have appeared in our lives. But this was a special call to share with Mom and Dad that we were pregnant with our second child and their seventh grandchild. Our new baby was due in mid-December and we wanted my parents to come to our home in Kirkland, Washington, instead of staying at their home in Las Vegas, Nevada.

Mom loved Christmas. With three daughters, no matter where we were living, we were all expected to be home for Christmas. And we wanted to be. It wasn't until life became complicated with marriages, moving away and new additions to each family, that we weren't able to get back home every year. For Mom to have to leave her home for Christmas was a big change from her usual Christmas festivities. Nonetheless, I knew she would be here for the birth of our new baby just like she was when our son, Max, was born.

As the months passed by, we talked about the trip and the amount of time she and Dad would stay. Of course, everything was planned around the arrival of, what we came to find out, would be our new little girl, Anna. I could hardly wait for them to spend Christmas with our small family. Christmas mornings were so much fun growing up, and I wanted Mom to see how I had recreated that same feeling here in my own home. I imagined our home beautifully decorated in traditional reds and greens with an ornament-covered Christmas tree, surrounded by presents reaching out from under its branches and extending across the living room. I wanted Mom to see how important her influence had been, and how much I'd learned from her.

During the first week of July, Mom called late one afternoon. She had been having pains in her side, and her doctor said she had gallstones. Mom assured me this was an easy fix, no problem. She was going to have a quick surgery to remove the gallstones and shortly thereafter, return to the golf course. Christmas was only six months away. Mom, just like me, starts counting the months until Christmas as soon as the new year begins. She carried the Christmas Spirit with her throughout the year, even keeping a sharp eye out for special gifts the entire twelve months on the calendar.

In mid-July, we found out it wasn't only the gall stones causing all the pain in Mom's side. Mom had cancer. There were suggestions for treatment options and lots of doctor appointments. My dad and my sister Ann, still living and raising her family in Las Vegas, took good care of her and made sure she was receiving the treatments she needed. My little sister, Teensie, flew in from Alabama to help take care of Mom. I still talked to Mom every day, and was hopeful the cancer would be eradicated.

By the middle of August, Mom was not improving. With my doctor's blessing, I flew down to Las Vegas to see her. That afternoon, Ann and I loaded her into the car and drove Mom to her oncology appointment. After peppering the doctor with questions, and not fully understanding what was going on, I finally realized he was telling us we had a very limited amount of time left to spend with Mom. I couldn't believe it. I don't even think Mom could believe it.

Mom's health continued to decline, and we were all devastated. In November, at eight months pregnant, sitting at my desk, I called Mom from work and asked her to fly to Seattle.

"Why do you want me to come up there?" she asked.

Unable to contain my sadness at the thought of losing her, I burst out crying "Because I don't want you to die." Struggling to stop the tears, I explained to her there was a doctor in Seattle that I thought she should see. A young girl in our office had spoken very highly of him. This doctor had found her mother's cancer when no one else could and saved her life. His care had brought her back from sure death. I wanted Mom to have the same opportunity.

So, on a rainy Thursday morning, just one week before Thanksgiving, Ann and Mom flew up. Mom came off the plane in a wheelchair with a small gold cross hanging around her neck. The cross surprised me. I had never seen her wear one before. As a matter of fact, we rarely went to church growing up and scarcely spoke of God. It was my grandmother, Mamaw, who planted the seeds of Christianity in me. Mom was Mamaw's daughter, and I wondered if perhaps those seeds were, somehow, now flourishing in Mom.

My heart sank as I watched Ann maneuvering Mom in her wheelchair through the crowds at the arrival gate. Mom had become thin and frail. She was no longer able to walk, and needed help getting in and out of the wheelchair. While this was certainly a physical change from August, she was still her usual self, in charge and smiling.

When we arrived at our house, there was a surprise waiting for Mom. Knowing she would not be back for Christmas, I had decorated our entire house with wreaths, garland, ornaments, and my own Christmas collections. Not one room in the house was left untouched. For Mom's bedroom, my husband Greg and I had purchased a live Christmas tree, a Korean Fir, and draped it with a swath of festive Christmas fabric, covering the water pan and black plastic container the tree was rooted in. The tree was brightly decorated and standing within her reach, making sure her room was full of merriment and Christmas cheer. I wanted

Mom to be surrounded by the love of her family and the Spirit of Christmas while she stayed with us. That Korean Fir was later planted outside and has been forever known as Mom's Tree.

Ann and I helped Mom upstairs and got her comfortably settled into her bed. Max, having just turned two, and not fully aware of Christmas quite yet, was simply thrilled to have his Gramma Bean, as we called her, sleeping in the room across the hall. He crawled up on his Gramma Bean's bed, drank her water through a straw and brought joy to Mom as only a grandchild could. She was very animated with Max and loved having him sit near her on the bed. Mom had always been unhappy that she couldn't see Max regularly. After Max was born, and Mom had gone back home, she called and said, "He will never know me." But he did know her. She was his Gramma Bean. And on this day, he made her laugh. Just for a moment, he took away the pain and the constant presence of the disease.

It was wonderful to have Mom at our home. My sister and I spent most of the afternoon sitting on her bed, entertaining Max, and talking about her wishes. Mom wanted to make sure, as she always had, that each of her three daughters was treated equally and gifted accordingly. She wanted us to decide right then and there, who would inherit each of her rings. This was a hard conversation for Ann and me because none of us girls cared about any of that. We just wanted our mom to live. However, Mom was preparing us for something we didn't want to face.

During a quiet moment, I asked her about the cross. Mom told me she had been visited by the son of a dear friend. He was a pastor, and they had prayed together. I wasn't exactly sure what had transpired during their visit, but something had been stirred because Mom was now wearing a cross. That was a seed Mamaw had planted, and Mom had just watered in me.

The next morning, Ann and I loaded Mom into the car and drove her to see the doctor. He was incredible with her. For the first time since all of this began, we had clarity on where the disease lived, what was happening and what we could expect. He told Mom to get her affairs in order. He also told Ann what she would need when they got back to Las Vegas. But, most importantly, he told all three of us that he believed in miracles, which gave us a little bit of hope. We all needed that. One way or another, it was the only positive thing we had to hang onto.

In the past, whenever Mom came up to visit, I would take her to two of my favorite places. They had become her favorite places as well. One was Molbak's Garden and Home store, and the other was a quaint little shopping area called Country Village. This trip was no exception, she wanted to go to both places.

Ann and I were thrilled, and carefully buckled Mom into the car to begin our adventure. We first went out to lunch at Country Village. At this point, Mom relied mostly on shakes and nutrient-enriched liquids, so the lunch was more for the three of us to have a normal activity and spend a little fun time together. But, after lunch, Mom was very tired and wanted to go back to my house. I was sad for her, knowing how much she loved Molbak's. She was looking forward to seeing the beautiful Christmas decorations, but she needed to rest. So, we loaded her back into the car and drove home.

Taking Ann and Mom back to the airport was hard. I wasn't sure when, and if, I would see Mom again. Baby Anna was due in three weeks. We had a new life coming into the world, and another life preparing to leave the world. We had a very happy occasion on the horizon, and an extremely sad moment at hand.

My doctor was fully aware of what was going on in my life. At the end of November, she told me Anna was "fully cooked" and we could induce labor in three weeks, right around her due date. That would allow Greg, Max, Anna, and me to fly to Las Vegas and see my mom, as she wanted to meet Anna. Looking back, I knew she was waiting for this birth. Mom was hanging on to meet her new granddaughter.

On the morning of December 14th, Greg and I went to the hospital to have our new baby girl. I had just been hooked up to the drip line when a nurse came in and said a man called the hospital and left a message for Greg to call him immediately. Greg left the room and came back a few minutes later.

He told me it was my dad. Recently Mom had been put on hospice care at home. She could no longer get out of bed. Mom was heavily drugged for the pain and spent most of her days in a deep sleep. Yet, this morning, the morning she knew Anna was to arrive, Mom was clearheaded. She woke up, sat up in bed, and asked for the newspaper so she could work on a crossword puzzle. Dad, on Mom's insistence, told Greg to call him every hour for an update on the birth. Greg did. He stepped out of the room and called hourly to assure my mom everything was okay.

At 9:42pm, Anna was born. Greg made his final phone call to Dad to give him the news. We found out later, as soon as Mom heard Anna was born, and I was fine, she slipped back into her deep, drug-induced sleep. She would remain like that for days.

My doctor arranged for me to have a private hospital room. The nursing staff must have known our goal was to get this new baby to her Gramma Bean, and they stopped at nothing to prepare Anna and me for the flight. Anna's pediatrician was also on board and made sure Anna was ready to go. He set up an appointment for us to take Anna to Children's Hospital and have her tested for jaundice. Anna passed with flying colors and both of us had the approval to get on a plane.

Five days after Anna was born, the four of us flew to Las Vegas. The trip was a little rough with a stopover in San Jose and a delayed flight, but we finally arrived and went straight to my parent's house.

Mom was sitting up in bed waiting for us. Once again, she had been clearheaded since waking up that morning. Mom had been doing crossword puzzles all day in anticipation of meeting her new granddaughter.

Holding Anna in my arms, I walked across the room to Mom's raised hospital bed, and carefully lowered Anna into her frail, outstretched arms. Mom pulled her new grandbaby close, looked at her and said, "She's beautiful."

Mom held Anna for as long as she could, then looked at me. I reached down and took her granddaughter from her embrace, understanding Mom's sorrow in leaving this earth without watching her grandchildren grow up. Greg, Max, and I were able to talk with Mom for a few minutes longer, until she began to slip back into her deep sleep. She had waited. She had held on, and she had met her newest grandbaby.

Mom's home looked beautiful. My sister, Ann, had done an incredible job of decorating the entire house for her. The Christmas Spirit was surrounding Mom, and comforting to the rest of us. In the living room stood Mom's white Christmas tree, perfectly positioned for her to see when she looked through the opening of her bedroom door. For the past few years, she had given up on live Christmas trees. Mom said they dried out too fast, and the artificial Christmas trees could be left up much longer. This proud tree, heavily flocked with white snow, was covered in red cardinals. Just what Mom had asked Ann to do. It was simple and beautiful.

Ann had given Mom such a wonderful gift by decorating the house. Tokens of love spread across Mom's bedroom. Ann draped yards of twine across the room with every card, note, and letter Mom had received. They were hung in a beautiful display of friendship. Ann made sure Mom knew who the cards were from as she attached each one with care. I'm sure Mom loved this. She hadn't been taking visitors for a few weeks, so these cards were a daily reminder that her friends and family loved her and were thinking of her. They were special presents.

For the next two days, we visited with Mom when she was awake, but most of the time, she was sleeping. We managed to have a few brief conversations and Mom was able to touch and see Max and Anna one last time. Saying goodbye was hard. I knew I'd see her again in Heaven, but letting go of her here on earth was so very sad.

We flew back home on December 21st and settled our little family into bed to begin our new life with the four of us. Knowing Max and Anna would never really know their Gramma Bean was heartbreaking. But it would be my job to keep that memory alive and tell them about all the seeds she planted in my life, so I could pass those seeds onto the two of them.

Two days later, on December 23rd at 6:00pm, the phone rang. Standing in the kitchen, I picked up the phone only to hear Ann's voice at the other end. Mom had died at 5:45pm, just minutes ago. Mom was sixty-three years young. Crying and unable to speak, I handed the phone to Greg. Even though I knew this was going to happen, the finality of it was heart-wrenching.

I woke up on December 25th, Christmas morning, determined to make it a happy day for my family. I wanted to continue to celebrate Mom's favorite day of the year for her. She loved watching all of us open the huge pile of gifts she had spent the year collecting. And she taught me that even if a box contained something as small as a pair of socks, it was one more gift to add to the excitement of Christmas morning. It didn't have to be expensive, it just had to be fun.

With the stockings filled to their tops and the empty plate of carrots and cookies left next to the fireplace, we were ready for our own Christmas morning. Piled high under the Christmas tree were boxes full of carefully chosen gifts, with a brightly colored tunnel toy set up for Max to see when he came in the room. Just as it had begun so many years ago for Ann, Teensie, and me, a Christmas morning smile crept across Max's face when he toddled into the room and saw his new tunnel toy and Santa's boxes spilling from under the tree.

Two days later, on December 27th, we gathered in Las Vegas to remember the woman that had taught us so much about life. The service and celebration of Mom's life were over in a flash. But the seeds she planted with her daughters would continue to grow and spread to be planted in the lives of her grandchildren.

A year after Mom died, I tracked down the pastor who had prayed with her. I told him who I was and why I was calling. I wanted to know about Mom's faith before she died. I needed to understand the gold cross around her neck. He was happy to share with me that they had prayed together and read Psalm 23, a Psalm of David. The pastor told me that Mom had accepted Jesus.

I found comfort that day and I finally knew the story of the cross around her neck. Now I knew where she was and who she was with.

Looking back at the time between that first phone call announcing the arrival of Anna's birth and the final days of Mom's life, I found many times and thoughts that brought both comfort and peace to me. Mom was given enough time to spend many days with her daughters. This allowed all of us to find a way to say goodbye. She was also able to spend time with Dad, the man she had been married to for forty-five years. Mom received, and saw, the gift of friendship through those that sat with her, sent her notes, and called her. Mom died in her own home, during her favorite time of the year, surrounded by the Spirit of Christmas and all its glory.

The seeds Mom planted live on. Christmas traditions have been born and bred into my own children. They know exactly who Gramma Bean is, and Max thinks he may even remember her. I talk to and about my mom, as though she were standing right next to me. I still ask her for advice. I still cry out for her. She will forever be a part of me and who I have become.

Because of my mom and her mom, Mamaw, the seed of faith has grown strong in my heart. My faith and my church are now a very important part of my life. That seed has also been passed onto Max and Anna. I will try to water that seed and help it grow, no matter what my age.

Mom's Christmas was quite a bit different than we thought it would be. I can only imagine what entering Heaven two days before the celebration of Christ's birth looked like for her. Although Mom was unable to come to my home for Christmas as originally planned, she made it home to Heaven just in time for her own Christmas. That picture fills my heart with joy.

I miss you, Mom. Thank you.

# Samantha Root

## Co-Founder of Lujo Commercial Cleaning/
## Owner of Your Real Estate Group, LLC

*H*eart Word: Striped / What's the worst thing that could happen in being myself; that no one will like me? Okay. Big deal. Let's face it, I have stripes. I am a Believer, but I am flawed. I have earned every stripe that I have and would not change them for the world. I don't want to be anyone else except me. Why? Because I am gifted with the ability to be so raw and real that others around me feel safe enough to open up and share some of their most vulnerable stories. It allows them to have at least one person in this world who doesn't judge and can relate to day-to-day struggles. If you are authentically you, then it is what it is. I have found that is the best way to live life, and it allows me to say it has attracted all the perfectly imperfect.

It's no coincidence that Samantha Root possesses goals and aspirations the size of Texas. The Texas native is the owner of Your Real Estate Group and recently launched Lujo Commercial Cleaning, a woman and minority-owned full-service commercial cleaning firm. In July of this year, Sam also accepted the role of District Director with Fathom Realty in the West Valley.

Sam has been a licensed Realtor for 14 years. She began her real estate career in Texas. For the past 12 years, she and her husband and three children have been Arizona residents.

It was also during this time that the Root clan grew from three to five children. Their ages are 19, 17, 15, 4 and 2. Three years ago, after making a family decision to stay permanently and not move back to Texas, she earned her Arizona Real Estate license.

Sam is an active member of WEMAR (West Valley Association for Realtors) and participates on its committees. She is a member of NAR (National Association of Realtors) and METROTEX (The Dallas Texas Association of Real Estate).

On the commercial real estate side, Sam is a member of AZCREW (she sits on the Professional Development Committee), IFMA, AZBL, and a past Board Member of BOMA (Building Owner and Management Association). She was an active committee chair for seven of the ten years she participated.

Away from work, Sam enjoys reading, cooking, and scrapbooking. She enjoys spending quality time with her family and friends.

A fun fact: Sam is a blogger and has been one for nine years. She started a website called JustWalkInFaith that was created to help inspire others to share their stories through her vulnerable writings. In addition to English, she is also fluent in Spanish.

# *Faith Driven. People Inspired.*

## By Samantha Root

It's one thing to talk about your life casually on a blog with a few followers or with a group of people you trust. It's quite another thing to share your story in a book. I didn't realize it would be this tough to do. Yet here we are, a couple of hours before the deadline, and I'm submitting my story for the first time. It's time to get real, and I'm ready to do it.

The only reason I am sharing my story is that I said to the Lord earlier this year, "Whatever you want me to do, regardless of how big or challenging the task is, I will do it without a fight." Note that I didn't promise Him I would do it without procrastinating. Because of Him, I am willing to share my story in its rawest form.

Fitting my life into one chapter of a book is like asking me to cram all five of my children, including two car seats and two dogs into a two-door car. It just ain't gonna happen.

After much prayer and anxiety on how to share my story, I decided to do it in true Sam fashion. I will be nothing less than my authentic self.

I'm sharing my story for the benefit of you, nobody else. Yes, you, the one person I know God wanted me to write these pages for. He knew that if I could show you it's possible, it would bring you the courage to follow your dreams.

The purpose of sharing my story is not to recommend you do what I did. That was hard work and probably unnecessary on many levels. But, that's my life story, and I'm proud of it. You don't need to write a book, leave a six-figure salary job, and start two companies simultaneously to be successful. There's no need to have three kids early on and then have two more children much later on. But that's MY story.

To achieve greatness, you'll need to get comfortably uncomfortable with your life and not settle for less. Don't be the status quo. Girllll, the world has way too many of those. Create your own pattern, but don't be timid. OWN every single stripe that belongs to you.

That's what I have done. While not perfect by any means, I sit here on the couch with my Lula leggings; having just moments ago realized they have a small hole next to my butt cheek. I think, "Oh my gosh, where have I gone wearing these things?" Back to my point.

I'm not perfect, but I'm worthy.

The pieces of my story I share with you today are meant to be digested in bits and pieces. Perfectly imperfect, remember?

It's time to dive in.

One particular day at the age of 8, I had a lemonade stand. As my mom had to leave the house for a little while, she gave me this kitchen timer. Each time it beeped, I would run inside and give my stepdad his medication. It was a lot of responsibility for a kid. He died of cancer when I was almost 9 years old. I miss him tremendously but know in my heart he is with me every time I see the moon, "la luna," in the sky. When my stepdad passed away, I was diagnosed with severe depression.

Years later, my mom found love again, and my brother Raul came to be. His dad passed away in a car accident before he was born, so my mom and I became a great mother-daughter duo to take care of him. All that trauma in a short period of time caused a lot of friction and resentment between my mom and me. Today, I am blessed to say we are closer than we have ever been. Why? Because I now understand she was doing the absolute best with what she was handed in life. It is easy to judge someone or be angry that they don't handle things the way "you would." Guess what? No one handles tough stuff perfect. Everyone handles it in a way that is right for them at that exact moment. It took me a while to learn this.

While all this was going on, my dad and stepmom had two kiddos of their own. So, I was a big sister with a pretty big age gap between my siblings and me. My brother Matthew and my sister Jessica are some of the most special people in my life. One of the best titles I have is sister.

You'd assume with all these kiddos floating around, it would be great birth control for me as a teenager. Bloop! It wasn't. Michael, my ex-husband and I dated from the time I was 14. Even up to this day, I joke that I have known him two-thirds of my life. WOW.

I got pregnant at 16 and had Tayler at 17. I was pregnant with Analesia at 18 and had her at 19. I then got pregnant with Hayden at 20 and had him at 21. YES, Michael is the dad of all of my first three kids. Now moving on ...

Early on, when people first met me and realized my kids belonged to me and not my mom or dad, they would say things like: "Why on earth are you keeping these kids? Why didn't you get rid of them? You are a slut. You are careless. You are a dummy."

I have always believed that if you talk the talk, then you need to walk the walk. That's why I have my three kids and didn't terminate any of the pregnancies. It was a personal decision I knew I would have to never change my mind on. It wasn't their fault I was their mom. But it was my responsibility to take care of them. I refused to prove the "young mom" statistics right.

One day at the mall when I was 16 and pregnant with Tayler, a mom stopped her daughter and grabbed her by the shoulders and looked straight at me. She said, "See! That is what happens when you have sex early! Don't be like her." She then walked away. I was stunned. My mom was with me and bought me a fake diamond ring. I always wore that as a shield, so I at least looked "legitimate" in society.

At the age of 21, I found myself divorced with three kids under the age of four. I filed for bankruptcy. I had nothing left except my kids and a personal drive that wouldn't quit.

As a mother, children give you purpose. You aren't allowed to NOT give your best for them. Failure was not and has never been an option when it comes to my children. Providing a roof over my children's heads and food was a top priority. I am a momma bear beast when it comes to them. Even at our lowest points and with heavy financial struggles, I didn't want them to be scared. So, I worked harder.

I look back now and realize they were my saving grace because had I not had them, then I don't know how that dark time would have panned out. Not only were there kiddos involved, it included a failed marriage, and all the emotions that came with it.

I have a strong work ethic. I have done everything from nail salon manager, Old Navy staff member, receptionist at an animal clinic, to new home sales assistant, and then later on became a Realtor. When I was a receptionist at an animal clinic, one of our clients asked if I wanted to get into new home sales. I started as an assistant and worked my way up to the top-producing sales-person for the builder I later worked for. I became a Realtor for a brokerage the builder, and I decided to start. I helped Hispanic homebuyers and sellers.

I can honestly say I have no idea how I got where I am today. An old boss of mine once told me, "Sam, God has a way of putting single moms under certain people's wings and will provide for them."

I found this to be true. I made less than what my basic bills were. However, month after month, we made it. Years later, I met my now-husband, Patrick. I had to let my home go when the market tanked. I was a Realtor at the time. He met me while I lived in a one-bedroom apartment with my kids. We called it an "adventure" while he called it a "how on earth…."

Time passed, and stability, age, wisdom, and a steady-paying job took place. Patrick and I had two kids together. Today, my kids' ages are 19, 17, 15, 4, and 2. I often hear, "You look so young!" I chuckle as my body thinks I am 70. I say that because my body has taken a toll physically for having kids so young and then again with the other two. I am only 36 on the surface but I have three types of arthritis, had an ovary removed a few years ago, no gallbladder, a stomach disorder that flares up every now and then, a degenerative bone thing (which I can't even pronounce), eye nerve issues, and a pooch that won't go away. Oh, don't forget stretch marks. Soon I will go in for a hysterectomy because the doctor found some cells he was worried about. Owning my "jankyness" for sure.

I firmly believe I would not be here today if not for my strong faith. My faith allowed me to realize my kids need me here with them. I am very much a vocalist when it comes to talking about depression. I live a fulfilling life despite having the diagnosis of depression. Just because I have depression doesn't mean I am depression. My name is Samantha "Sam."

Depression doesn't make someone a loser, crazy, or inadequate. It does make you a hero, though. Every single day you are making a choice to live life. You are choosing to breathe one more day and take NO off the table. You are a hero even when your depression may keep you under the covers or living like a hermit. Depression comes and goes. If you have depression, always make sure you have a tribe around you that will pull you out from the blankets if you can't do it alone. I have a solid few friends that never make me feel crazy or defective.

My faith isn't unwavering. There was a point in my life where I hated God. Being a single teen mom struggling with babies wasn't easy. That all changed one day while I was crying in my closet. That is a whole other story for another time; how I came to find my faith and shop for a church.

The truth is we are all struggling to survive. Every day brings something new. I just keep moving. If I stop to think of where I have been and where I am at, I would cry and get overwhelmed. A counselor once told me that I had been a mother longer than I have not. That was EYE OPENING.

Now for the business side of things. I often hear the question, "How on earth do you have five kids and own two companies?" I respond, "Because I am a hot mess!"

My faith, being a mother, wife, and strong work ethic keep me going. Today I'm an entrepreneur running a commercial cleaning business in a male-dominated industry. I never thought I'd be doing this as I thought I had found my perfect job. It was until it wasn't. After working extremely hard for three years for a company I believed in, I became the CEO earning a six-figure salary.

The owner often commented that I had the most integrity of anyone he had ever met, even when it drove him crazy that I was so adamant always to do the right thing regardless of how hard that was. During this time, I sacrificed my family for the title of CEO. I won't lie, being acknowledged as CEO made me feel important. But then something happened that was very humbling and heartbreaking.

A change in ownership vision, and me not being able to compromise what I believed to be the right thing to do, caused company change. Besides losing the CEO title, there were other challenges. I had to deal with demotion, losing what I considered a best friend, and rebuilding my shattered self-esteem. I didn't understand, as even the owner agreed, I loved the company like it was my own. It was such a confusing and mind-damaging time. It came down to he was the owner of his business, and I was not.

This change happened within a couple months. BIG changes and BIG heartbreak do not go well together. I stayed at that company for a little while longer until the truth of what the situation was hit me like a two-by-four. I was not willing to compromise my belief and integrity. They couldn't pay me enough to do that. I was so depressed. I woke up every single day for two months feeling like I was in a daze. I felt like I had absolutely ZERO sense of purpose. I struggled daily to function. I cried, and my heart hurt. I realized working in a transactional position rather than as a leader was one of the worst things that could happen to someone that was wired like me. It was the beginning of the end. My heart stopped caring. I felt like a piece of trash and no longer loved where I was.

After going through some severe depression, I realized while working for this company, I forgot WHO I WAS. I see now this was divine intervention. It was time to find myself. I now saw I had a legacy to build! And this legacy would involve being an actual business owner. It's okay to be perfectly imperfect. Just because I am "emotional" doesn't take away that I am intelligent. Notice I didn't say smart. I said intelligent because I know I am. I can run a business without cracking a whip. I can run a company in Converse shoes just as easy as in a dress.

As a "depressed" woman with ambition and drive, I quit on the spot one day. I went from a six-figure income to zero. Y'all, it was a freaking awesome and peaceful feeling! Zero fear. I knew the Lord would provide for me because I was following what He had in store for me.

True to form, right away, my problem was solved. I started Lujo Commercial Cleaning with a business partner I have known for a decade. We are both known in the industry for integrity, ambition, and being family driven. Our company's motto is, "Always do the right thing no matter what."

In our business, there are no titles such as CEO. It doesn't matter what job you have. Just be the best at it. Failure isn't an option, but part of the not failing means you need to make a dent in the world in everything you do. That's why I stand up so much for my cleaners. Yes, they scrub toilets, but they have a servant's heart and are working for a reason.

I also took my real estate business full-time. I have been a licensed Realtor for 14 years, and have helped so many families buy and sell homes during that time. My purpose in life is to help others achieve what they never thought possible. For many, that dream is buying a home. I live to help others create memories and put their trust in me. The motto: Faith Driven. People Inspired also drives Your Real Estate Group (YRG).

I make it a point to do good in the community on behalf of the companies I work for because giving back is so important. I usually take my family with me. Today, I am proud to be me and am present in everything I do.

I run companies where I can believe in what we stand for. I have been chosen to run businesses that are legacy bridges. I do business with who I want to. I don't have to fight for what is right. I smile every single time I see the logos. I don't hide who I am to appease or keep my job. With pride, I tell people the company slogans are Faith Driven. People Inspired. If that scares you upfront, you won't like me at all.

I am not a Bible-thumper. Heck, the only scripture I have memorized is Psalm 46:10, "Be still, and know I am God." I am, however, called to bring other people together and create a space where they feel vulnerable enough to be authentic and loved without judgement.

Today, I am at complete PEACE. The peace I found brings me happiness.

For anyone who can relate and is moved by the story I've just shared, let's connect. I'm all over social media and love making new friends.

# *Tracy O'Malley*

**Founder and CEO of O'Malley Enterprises**
**Performance Coach, Enneagram Expert,**
**Author, Speaker/Founder, Strive 4 Change, LLC**

*H*eart Word: Bulletproof / You will need to stand on the front line of your life to have what you want. Take the hits required. Stand tall and proud, even after you get knocked on your ass, and let your God-given gifts shine.

Tracy O'Malley is a sought after powerhouse entrepreneur, mentor, speaker, author, and has been trained by the very best in the field. Coaching tens of thousands in her business mastermind and brainchild, Strive 4 Change, LLC, she has inspired over 60,000 to reach physical and financial freedom and transform their lives. As a motivational keynote speaker, industry leader, and top income earner, Tracy has shared her raw and real story and has encouraged her followers to smash their masks and live their true, authentic selves in pursuit of a higher level of living. Having earned many accolades and awards, Tracy has mentored 50+ six-figure income earners in her organization.

Tracy has recently expanded her entrepreneur spectrum with her latest venture consisting of group, online, and one-on-one coaching through her personally developed programs via web, workshops, and retreats.

As a single mother, Tracy raised two incredible grown children who are also finding enormous success in the entrepreneurial world. She also takes immense pride in her fur babies, rescuing two blue nose Pitbulls, Wrigley and Ivy. Tracy enjoys yoga, meditation, reading, and working out regularly. Being an Arizona transplant from Chicago, Tracy loves the Cubbies, hiking, and all things outdoors.

Tracy believes that we should never underestimate the power one decision to change your life can have.

How do you view your life? Is it something you trudge through, doing your best to survive? Or, is it a gift you value, pushing yourself beyond what is comfortable in order to be healthy, grow, and share your light with others?

# Becoming Bulletproof
### By Tracy O'Malley

Becoming bulletproof was something I wanted, but in reality, I didn't fully understand what it meant. I thought it meant being invincible where no one could hurt me. I wanted to find a way to make that possible. It started with that first drink when I was 15. While most kids my age selected a fruity wine cooler or Zima, not me. I chose Southern Comfort, a smooth-drinking whiskey. From that first drink, I knew I drank differently than the others. The minute it hit my lips, I felt an instant calm. It was like hitting that little steam release button on the top of the Instant Pot. The pressure was gone, and I felt instant relief. That is exactly how I felt the very first time I took a drink. The second, third, and fourth time didn't give the same kind of reprieve. So, I spent the next 25 years chasing that first-drink feeling. Just a heads up: I never found that again in a bottle, but I searched for it.

The night of my first drink, I drank the entire bottle of Southern Comfort. I don't recall much about that night, but I do recall the insane liquid courage it gave this soft-spoken, but edgy girl. I felt invincible and unstoppable. Nobody was going to hurt, touch, or control me. I felt bulletproof—if just for a moment in time. The next morning, I didn't feel so invincible. I was beyond sick. I blacked out the first time I drank. I prided myself on always being in control. With blackouts, you give up all that control in an instant. But, at times, to gain some relief, I soon learned I was willing to pay the price.

My dad was a high-functioning alcoholic. He never missed a day of work, but he was a Dr. Jekyll and Mr. Hyde kind of guy. I never knew what he'd be like when he came home. It was like

*144*

constantly walking on eggshells. All I knew was that I was never going to be like him, but as a family we kind of normalized it. At age 4, you can see me in a photo with my dad passed out in the recliner. Obviously drunk, you can see the glass of whiskey and the lit cigarette beside him. I am standing in front of my dad with a big smile on my face with my hands in a position that's like, "Nothing to see here. We're good, we're good." Looking back, I was the kid that nobody worried about because I was so quiet and attempted to take care of everything. Let me remind you, I was doing that at age 4.

Pain was inevitable in our household. Once I discovered alcohol, I knew how to escape pain. Sometimes, while in high school, I would drive intoxicated. By the grace of God, I didn't hurt myself or anybody else. One time at age 17, I was blitzed beyond belief. I ended up being passed around between two guys at a party and was sexually assaulted as a result.

But, here's the worst part, I thought I imagined the entire night. I was sleeping in our living room on the recliner when I woke up. I opened my eyes and thought, "Thank God, that was just a dream." I then looked over to my right. The dirty, mud-stained clothes I was wearing the night before were splattered across the floor. I rushed outside as I wasn't sure how I got home. And sure enough, I parked my pickup truck like a boss in its parking spot which was scary in and of itself. Thank God there were angels watching over me that night. The problem was, I never felt worthy of that kind of love or grace.

Alcohol played a significant role in my life. It allowed me to not feel my feelings, suppress them, and feel safe. I thought that was the definition of bulletproof. It wasn't. Shame was always right there by my side. Shame is the silent killer because it will rob you of everything you desire and dream about. Nobody wants to feel the shame. Shame hurts. It's a wicked, vicious cycle. Shame will stop you dead in your tracks on the way to a breakthrough. We go back to what makes us not feel the shame which perpetuates the behavior that keeps the madness going. Rinse and Repeat puts us more into shame. I believe that's why I continued drinking for 25 years. For me, I didn't think I had a problem because I didn't drink or desire it every day. I kept saying, "I'm not an alcoholic. I don't have a problem because I'm not like my dad."

I come from a big Irish family so by birthright I was born to drink and fight like that. That's part of the Irish DNA code. When I was pregnant, I didn't drink at all and rarely drank when my kids were little. But, as I got older and problems started in my marriage and I didn't think the kids were as impressionable, I would drink when they weren't around. They didn't see me drinking until they were in junior high and high school. They didn't even realize that it was an issue for me until then. To compensate during this time when I wasn't drinking, my hibernating eating disorder kicked back into overdrive. I would bounce between anorexia and bulimia. The act of bulimia is vile, but it was the greatest high I've ever had. It was so symbolic of everything I wanted for my life. The idea was to stuff the feelings so far down it hurt, and when it hurts, you just get rid of it.

This eating disorder did the trick as I'd stuff the feelings inside with as much food as possible. And then just like the Instant Pot with the steam release button, I'd let it go. There was nothing better as I physically got to see what I was letting go. I justified all of this because in my mind it wasn't hurting anybody but me. This is a lie, however, that's how I made it okay in my head and kept it a secret. With the eating disorder, I was able to function and it created a lot less wreckage than alcohol. I thought this was what it meant to be bulletproof. I was wrong. It was my way of being bulletproof.

When I got divorced and explored dating as an adult for the first time, it was really awkward and I was socially uncomfortable. And that's when I started my high-level drinking again. Coupled with the eating disorder, I was being tag teamed by two powerhouses that had a strong hold on me. It was just a matter of time before one of them tore me in two. It was the highest high. Alcohol was like throwing gasoline on a smoldering fire.

Since then I've discovered you can take away the alcohol and the food addictions, but underneath it all is this desire to feel connection, relieve the pain, and to feel safe. If you don't know why you are using food or alcohol in this way, you are going to fill that need with something else. The things we lean into are just the symptom of something missing—something bigger.

I've had a lot of pain in my life. Pain is inevitable for all of us, but I think sometimes we just want to avoid it. Pain is just a symptom of a lack of connection to something safe and having no instruction manual for how to deal with it.

For about 15 years, I was in the car transport industry. At first I was an owner of a car transport company. When I got a divorce, I decided to close the door on that venture, eventually leaving the industry. I then went into the corporate side. My drinking accelerated at a rapid pace and got completely out of control at this point. It wasn't just situational anymore—it was everyday survival. As a single mom who wasn't receiving any child support, I was the sole provider.

At age 40, I knew something had to change, but I didn't see a way out. When you feel like you are trapped and do not see an end in sight, you become hopeless. At that point in my life, I felt hopeless. That's why I drank as much as I did during that time. I felt like this was as good as it was gonna get. As I was telling my kids who were 14 and 15 at the time that they can be or do anything they wanted in life, I was showing them something completely different. Unfortunately, I was very aware that kids do what their parents do, not what they say to do. Considering my dad's situation, I was living proof of it.

In the summer of 2012, I got a call from my dad. By the tone of his voice, I could tell it was serious. My dad was the man of no filters, so I knew some brutal truth was coming. He had just been diagnosed with cancer and the doctors didn't give him much time to live. I said, "Okay dad, give me the bottom line. What does that mean?" He had three weeks to three months to live. Eleven days later, my uncle called to tell me that hospice had just been called in. Leaving my desk, my life in shambles, which was how every day felt, I bolted as fast as I could in hopes to make it back home to see him before his time on earth was done. On the flight back to Chicago to see my dying dad, I was really angry, not because he was dying, as I knew he was in God's hands, but because I felt trapped and controlled by a situation and job I didn't like. During the duration of that flight back home, I prayed, a snot-bubble ugly kind of prayer for an opportunity to do something different with my life.

Twelve days after my dad's phone call, he passed away. At this point, I had stopped drinking and had about 30 days of the "dry life" sobriety under my belt. I made it through for another six weeks, but I was a shell of a person. After he passed away, I realized how cruel the cliché that life was too short and tomorrow is never guaranteed could be.

I didn't have an instruction manual on how to deal with the pain of grief, or anything for that matter, so I turned to something that I knew would make me feel better, maybe even bulletproof. At the time, my boyfriend was a dysfunctional drinker, an alcoholic just like my dad. He said, "What's one weekend of drinking going to do? Let's go to Vegas." Instead of sitting through this pain,

I chose the getaway. While there, I experienced the worst blackout of my life. It was messy, it was ugly, and left a shit ton of wreckage behind. I realized after that I needed help badly. I quit drinking again. This time, for good.

That's when my anorexia got passed the baton. For three weeks, dealing with the shame, guilt, grief, and pain, I didn't eat a morsel and I lost 25 pounds. While lying on the kitchen floor, I knew I had two options. Die right there or ask for help. By through the grace of God, I chose to ask for help. I called my uncle and said, "I need help." This was the man who was there for me when I was sexually assaulted at age 10. This was the man that pulled me out of our home when it got ugly and let me be a kid. This was a man that saw who I was, even when I masked it. He assured me I could beat this, that I was better than this. I also talked to a friend with four years of sobriety under her belt and asked for direction. There was no mistaking it, I was going to rehab. If I didn't get out of my environment fast, it would just be a matter of time before I was back to what I knew.

The day before going into rehab, I quit the job I hated. I walked into the owner's office and said, "I'm going to leave and I'm not coming back because if I come back it's just a matter of time before I die. I don't want any fanfare and I'm going to leave quietly. I'm not going to say goodbye to anybody. Just gonna pack my desk and go and I'm not coming back." That day I took my income down to zero with no real safety net. That night, I sat my kids down and said, "I don't know how we're gonna be okay, but I know why we will. I'm gonna give this everything I've got." My son who was 14 at the time said, "We'll give you up for 30 days to have you the rest of our life."

While in rehab from alcohol, I revealed my eating disorder which I kept a very big secret from everyone. I knew that if I didn't put all the cards on the table, it was just a matter of time before I went back to my eating disorder. And that was going to take me out way faster than alcohol ever did because I was so destructive with it. Most people can't readily hide when they've got an alcohol problem, but you can hide a problem with food very easily if you're pretty slick and manipulative like I was. I thought this was the right path to being bulletproof. It wasn't.

While in inpatient rehab, I realized it was easy to be sober while in the sage confines of that environment. But when I came back home, back to the reality I created, I realized I needed to change everything. So, I wiped out my entire social network, damn near every friend, and the love of my life. Headhunters were calling me from the car industry because I was really good at what I did.

I recall sitting in job interviews and people offering me tons of money when I was down to almost nothing, totally broke. But, I couldn't follow through with it. At one point, I stopped somebody halfway through the interview and said, "I apologize for wasting your time, but I am coming out of my skin at the thought of doing this job. It's nothing personal, it's just I know there's a bigger calling in my life." That took guts. A lot of it. I was a woman that thrived on certainty and control, and yet something felt so right about honoring that decision.

A few weeks later, I was introduced to the network marketing industry by accident. I began with a product, I fell in love with it, only to realize it was "one of those things." It was the last thing I wanted to do, but then I remembered back to being on the airplane praying for an opportunity to do something different when my dad was in his final moments. On my six-month sobriety date, my prayer was answered through network marketing. I didn't like God's answer to my prayer at all. I was like, "God, this is not what I meant by an opportunity to do something different. I am not the poster child of health and wellness. I'm a single mom who just went to rehab." But God had something bigger in mind. I soon realized this was a stepping- stone for a greater calling. Through this opportunity, I learned how to build a community from ground zero as I had no social network at that point. In two years, I took my network marketing business from zero to a million-dollar income. I was crushing it and helping thousands of people along the way. My ego particularly loved the "crushing it" part. Today, that organization stands 95,000 people strong. Despite my success, I wasn't always thriving in that environment. I had to take a step back from my business when, unexpectedly, my health started to decline and there were no ready answers. Meanwhile, my business grew which showed me that I knew how to build leaders. I realized I was coaching my team not networking marketing skills, but self-awareness tools, radical honesty, and skills they could use in every aspect of their life. This kept them in the game with me, and in a way also held me accountable.

When I was in rehab, I took this personality test to understand myself and the way I communicated. I also wanted to see what my career calling might be. I discovered the Enneagram of Personality types and was fascinated by the complexity of it. To me, it felt like a huge jigsaw puzzle with so many moving parts. I loved it. I was a little mortified when I discovered my personality type. On the Enneagram, I am known as The Challenger (an 8). As is human nature, I looked right at all the unhealthy traits of this personality type. As I sneaked a peek at the different themes, words jumped out to me like intensity, secrecy, withdrawal, control, and manipulation.

Instead of being discouraged and focusing on what I didn't like about my personality, I looked at all the positive traits of my personality type. I had the traits of a fierce, powerful leader that could move the needle faster than any other leaders. I was trustworthy and had credibility. I could be outspoken, yet respectfully direct, bold with confidence, decisive, tough, and compassionate.

Although I wasn't quite checking all of those boxes yet, I knew it was just a matter of time before I was. Like a G.P.S. System, I kept my eyes on where I was headed. My personality became like a compass as it helped guide me. Sometimes I'd go off the road a bit, but with the tools of the Enneagram, I knew it wasn't something I needed to beat myself up for. Instead, I knew I just needed to, and then pivot to course-correct.

The Enneagram taught me that being self-aware saves you from the inevitable shame that goes along with whatever is holding you back. Transforming your life is possible if you are self-aware. But, here's the thing, to become self-aware, you need to learn to slow down. I didn't think slowing down was an option for me until I got so sick. Doctors could not figure out what was wrong with me. After 14 specialists, they were able to nail it down and assign me a very humbling protocol. For 16 weeks, I sat in my recliner every single day for eight hours. It was almost like it was God's way and my body's way of saying, "We've got something much bigger for you. Oh honey, you aren't even getting started yet." In the end, I was diagnosed with late stage chronic Lyme Disease, something that is so misunderstood and hard to battle. But in the battle, I found the blessings.

This was the wake-up call I needed to go after that life I've always wanted. I was about to embark on a coaching business that could help others break through the barriers that have been holding them back. The Enneagram of Personality has become the biggest self-awareness tool for me and is what I share with my clients. Now, I've become more self-aware than anyone I've ever met in my life. I teach people the awareness piece, and of course, because it is human nature, everyone goes to the negative aspects of their personality. And with my guidance, I share ways they can transform their lives. I also help them acknowledge where it all stems from, and of course give them tools to integrate everything they learn in real time. The fact is, I can accelerate transformation in others faster than most people because of all the work I've done and continue to do on myself, as well as the thousands of others I have helped do the same.

We are all capable of transforming our lives. To do so, you must be willing to stand at the front line of your life and take the hits. Even when you get knocked on your ass, which you will, know you can get back up and face everything life has to offer, not just the pain, but the joy. It's time to live your life like a human being, not a human doing.

The last four months of my life have hands down been the hardest. There have been deaths of some of the most influential people in my life, family dynamic changes that were beyond hurtful, new plot twists, my personal safety threatened, and loss of family pets. Just one of these things a decade ago would have had the power to derail me, or even kill me. I have had to face hard conversations and situations head-on. For starters, the man who did my father's eulogy passed away from cancer. He was the one who told me, "You are better than this. Your calling in life is so much bigger than what you've been doing." My uncle who was always there for me died, then almost four months to the day, his sister, my aunt, died. She was a big part of my childhood and was my role model of a strong single mom. As a result of these deaths, I've had to put myself in uncomfortable environments and situations with my family who have disowned me. But, I've been able to do it. And that is what becoming bulletproof is all about. It's knowing I can put myself in any situation and be bulletproof. It's knowing that regardless of the situation I am put in, and regardless of the pain that needs to be endured, I am bulletproof.

The last few months have knocked me on my ass but I get back up and I'm stronger and better and more grateful because of it. I'm not angry and I'm not a victim. I understand that this is all part of the process and for the greater good. If there's nobody teaching us how to handle life we're going to have a world full of people not living the life they were supposed to live. Many will attempt to numb it out, stuff it down, or put themselves in situations that aren't best for them. I know this, because I have done it and have spoken with thousands of others that have, too. We live in a world where people tend to treat the symptom, not the underlying issue. That is what has been modeled, told, and taught. If it isn't repaired, it is repeated. We need to get to the root of the problem. If you don't pull weeds up by the root, they are going to grow back bigger, stronger, and faster. When you pull them up by the roots, it takes a lot longer for them to come back and invade your space.

Being bulletproof is better. It doesn't mean you don't feel. Ask anybody in law enforcement that's worn a bulletproof jacket and actually taken a hit from a bullet. It hurts and leaves bruises. But, they're able to get back up again. I think about what I did when I stopped drinking and went to rehab. It was the first step of many. I knew that if you don't repair it, then you repeat it. When I started this self-exploration journey, I so badly didn't want to pass this onto my kids and I almost did. I remember looking at my daughter when she was four years old. I recognized myself in her at that age. By the grace of God and a relentless and unstoppable desire to do the work to change, generational patterns of addiction, codependency, and a truckload of other things stopped with me. Now my kids don't have to carry that burden, and the generations after me won't either. I've changed the legacy of my family and I want to help others do the same. That's what being bulletproof is all about.

# Mayra Hawkins

**Spiritual Coach and Founder of
Women Who Mean Business AZ**

*H*eart Word: Optimistic / There is always a new canvas in front of us where we can create a new possibility for the future!

I am the Founder of Women Who Mean Business AZ. I am also a Certified Life Coach with The Life Mastery Institute and the Owner of The Leap to Transformation, LLC.

I spent 30 years of my life in the corporate world in the banking and financial industry. These long years provided me with the experience and the knowledge to help others navigate and deal with their financial matters, both in their businesses and personal lives. My life experience, the stories, the tears, and the wisdom my clients shared with me, motivated me to become a Life Coach.

Based on my own personal journey, I am able to relate and help others navigate through their difficult times and setbacks. I have learned many lessons through bankruptcy, divorce, and motherhood. Today, my passion is to share my knowledge and pearls of wisdom with others to empower and motivate them. My ideal client is a female entrepreneur or a woman in transition. I help them gain the clarity needed to release their fears and align with the invisible side of success. I coach and guide them to stay connected to their passion and their vision so they don't give up on their dreams.

# There's Got to Be Something Bigger and Greater Out There

### By Mayra Hawkins

At the age of 4, I became a motherless daughter. It was the beginning of a lifetime filled with sorrow, missing my mommy, and yearning for the love and attention of a father who was not always present. As I began to navigate through the side effects of abandonment and all the fears associated with it, life unraveled in unexpected turns for me.

It is fascinating how, at such an early age, our brains begin to create the genesis of our identity. Somehow, I still have the vision or the image of my mom leaving for the hospital with my dad waving goodbye at me. She was wearing a black dress and her beautiful smile. After they left, I remember gathering some flowers from our garden so I could give them to her after she got back. Sadly, she never came back. She was only 28 years old when she passed away. This was the beginning of my journey.

My intention as I share this writing with you is to help both of us heal. I want to inspire you to take action when you feel powerless and to encourage you to continue to grow and practice discernment. I want to remind you to give thanks for all the experiences that brought you to this moment, and to never lose yourself and give your power away. The circumstances in our lives can often derail many of us from our dreams or keep us stuck in victimhood. It is important to know that as long as we are breathing, we can create new possibilities for ourselves and make a greater impact on the lives of others.

I was born and raised in Puerto Rico, in the town of Ponce. It is the second-largest city on the island. After losing my precious mother, our family broke apart for a while. My father had to work and could not take care of us, so my sister and I went to live with my Aunt Raquel, and my little brother, who was only a year old, went to live with my Aunt Vickie. After a short time, we were reunited again and moved to my Great Aunt Angie's house. She became a mother figure to me. She gave us pure and unconditional love. She would take me to the corner store to get candy and would let me brush her hair while she took a nap. She taught me how to make scrambled eggs, how to sew the hem of my skirt, and how to iron perfect pleats. I was raised Catholic, so she also taught me the meaning of prayer, and how to use the rosary to connect with God—the invisible power that would listen and comfort me when I was sad and lonely. Sort of like my imaginary friend. I would ask God to deal with the monsters under my bed and keep me safe in the dark. As an innocent little girl, I tried to make sense of it all. I did everything I could to have joy and create happiness around me.

As my mother died very young, I'm sure it was devastating for my father to lose her. She was a beautiful woman, and I imagine she was very naive about men. My dad was not always around. I don't recall spending much time with him. I vaguely remember arguments between them where he would take off in the car and leave her in tears. Later, I learned that he was actually married to another woman. He never actually married my mother. Regardless, I'm sure that he loved her very much. After all, they had three kids together, and he gave us his name. My mother died in 1965 from complications from an abortion. I assume that based on guilt, my father promised her that he would always protect us before she died.

By the age of 6, I had my first stepmother. She was another beautiful young woman who had no business raising someone else's children. All she did was drink, party, and argue with my father. It was very confusing for me. Their relationship didn't last very long. Very soon after, we were introduced to our second step-mother. I remember our dad requesting that we call her "mom," and I was not too happy about that. She was not my mother! We became an instant Brady Bunch family with a new stepsister, another little sister on the way, and one more little brother later on. We were now a party of eight! To this day, everyone is still in my life, and I love them all very much.

My teen years were a living hell from my point of view. There was never money to do anything, no fun, no love, and no under-standing. We were never allowed to go out with friends to mov-ies, the mall, or anywhere alone. Our entertainment consisted of watching TV in black and white, of course! It was almost like being in prison. We were constantly doing chores around the house and dealing with my stepmother drinking in the evenings. I imagine that she was very lonely and sad, too. My dad would come home late at night drunk, and she would start screaming at him about the lipstick on his white shirts or the smell of perfume. Many times we would wake up in the middle of the night to wit-ness their domestic violence episodes. I recall her leaving several times and flying to the US to be with her sister in Chicago. All of those times were filled with fear and sadness for the future. We had very little love and nurturing from our parents, and I often felt like running away.

At the age of 13, I met my first boyfriend. He was 17, tall, and handsome. I could only see him during my trips to the corner store a couple of times a week. I was very happy, and everything was so perfect until my father found out. He then forbid me to see him for no particular reason other than being protective of me. I was devastated, so much that I attempted to end my life by taking a bunch of pills. The next morning I remember feeling extremely sick and throwing up. I never did tell my parents or anyone what

exactly happened. I was terrified about the consequences if anyone found out. I had mixed feelings and felt really sad afterwards.
Obviously, God had better plans for me. Later, when I turned 15,
my father finally allowed him to come to visit me once a week in
our home. That was our entire dating life for the next three years.

The same young boy I nearly killed myself over and was for-
bidden to see at one point, became my first husband when I turned
18. I remember sneaking out of the house one morning and writing a sad letter to my dad. I don't exactly recall what I said, but
something about the fact that I was running away because I didn't
want to follow his rules any longer. I wanted to be with the love
of my life full time and be his wife! I was all grown up and knew
exactly what I was doing! It was actually bittersweet.

We eloped with the help of my first boss, Gloria. I had worked
for her since the age of 14. She treated me like a daughter and
often didn't agree with the way my father raised me. She knew
I wanted to move out of my home, so she helped me with my
plan to escape. Then one day, early in the morning, she picked me
up, and we went to her house to change into my rented wedding
gown. I was really nervous and afraid that I would get caught. We
then drove to a small church in the neighborhood and had a very
intimate wedding ceremony at 7:00 am. There were only six of us
and a few old ladies from the neighborhood. There were no wedding invitations, and obviously, my family was not there. We then
drove to San Juan, stayed one night, and then flew to St. Thomas
the next day for our blissful honeymoon. It was the best time of
my life! It was finally time for my happily ever after!

Two years later, we were blessed with the birth of our little girl.
It was the best feeling in the world to be a mother. She was so perfect and precious. My world was complete now. I didn't like leaving her at the babysitter after 45 days to go back to work, but my
husband didn't have a stable job at the time. Soon after, he decided

to join the U.S. Coast Guard. He was sent away for almost a year to complete his training and then attend culinary school. After he got back, he received his orders, and we moved to the US.

It was tough for me to be in a new country away from my family and my culture. At that time, I barely spoke English and didn't know how to drive a car. My husband was always gone on duty on the ship—sometimes for 45 days at a time at sea. I spent endless days and nights waiting for him and watching telenovelas at home. During this time, I tried to make friends with some of my neighbors. I was very naive and trusted everyone at the time. One night before my husband was due back from the sea, I invited some friends over for dinner. A simple evening with friends turned out to be the worst nightmare of my life. My neighbor, who drank a little too much, tried to kiss me and I ended up with a big hickey on my neck. I was terrified knowing that I would have to explain this mess to my husband the next day.

When my husband arrived the next morning, he saw the mark on my neck and got extremely upset and violent with me. He tried to kill me while I was still holding our two-year-old baby in my arms. I remember screaming, but no one could hear me. This was terrifying to my daughter and me. We were both crying hysterically. He continued to scream at me and threaten me again by telling me that he was going to come back with his gun and to be ready to face the consequences. Then he left.

I didn't know what to do. I ended up calling the same neighbor to ask for help as I yelled and blamed him for being the cause of my despair. All I knew then was that I needed to leave and protect myself and my daughter. The pain and the shock of this experience left me traumatized and very confused. I was able to stay in a hotel at the military base until friends from church got involved and tried to help, but reconciliation was not an option for me. I realized that this was the end of my happily ever after. Shortly after, I moved away with my two-year-old daughter to upstate New York to be with my older sister.

After this horrific experience, two years later, I ended up marrying the same stupid neighbor. He was the same guy who destroyed my marriage and then rescued me from the worst nightmare of my life. I was only 24 years old at the time. Yes, this is called insanity! The marriage ended very quickly after I found out that he was only separated from his wife but never legally divorced. I was very naive, and he was definitely a smooth operator and a big liar.

Life works in mysterious ways. I can't imagine why I would want to get married again, but I did. Actually, three more times! Since I was so young, I kept dreaming of having more children, so I continued to search for someone who would fulfill this dream and build a life with me. After many prayers, I met a man in a military uniform who swept me off my feet. Six months into the relationship, he asked me to marry him. He then introduced me to his family. We then went to the justice of the peace, and it was done! Later on, I discovered that he was an atheist, and our relationship started to go sideways. As someone who was raised Catholic, I didn't want to raise my daughter with different values, so this created many arguments between us. He was also verbally abusive to me. By then, we were living in Arizona. A year later, he was discharged from the military due to his bizarre behavior. I remember him writing messages on dollar bills and crossing over "in God we trust" with a sharpie pen. He then moved away to Florida to find work with his brother. And there I was, alone again! I decided to move in with a coworker and shortly after, I filed for divorce. I was glad I did.

Through these divorces, I have endured tons of confusion, despair, loss, pain, tears, and mostly shame. I also experienced many years of counseling and suffering with my daughter as she was affected as much, or even worse, than me. Somehow, I learned to cope with the complexity of it all and roll with the punches. I have learned to live with the judgment and misunderstandings of many, knowing that they haven't walked in my shoes.

My journey to Arizona landed me my first job in the banking industry. I was blessed to be able to build a career from scratch. I barely had a GED when I applied for the job, and my English was not perfect. When I was given the opportunity to become a teller, I was so excited. I did my very best and created a foundation for advancing in the industry. I took advantage of every opportunity. I managed to excel quickly and soon was promoted to personal banker. I learned to open accounts, help my clients balance their checkbooks, and teach them about saving for the future. I remember wanting to learn more. I always took the initiative to educate myself on something new. I observed the way people dressed and talked around me. My goal was to become a branch manager one day.

I worked for Bank of America for many years, and throughout my career, I encountered many managers who were able to see my potential and encouraged me to go further and stretch. My first big leap of faith was learning how to process mortgage loans. It was difficult to learn the new jargon, but it was exciting for me when I got my certificate and passed all my courses! I was ready to help more people build their dream of homeownership. I always wanted to make a difference in people's lives. This opportunity was extremely rewarding. Later, I also became a volunteer with Habitat for Humanity and was privileged to serve on their Board for many years. It really put into perspective the true meaning of homeownership for me.

In 2000, one of those managers who had always believed in me opened a bank and invited me to join his team. Without any hesitation, I accepted the offer. It was the best thing I ever did for my banking career. I achieved my dream of becoming a branch manager. My future was bright, and the market was hot! We exceeded our goals year after year. I continued to raise the bar for myself. I then went on to study and got some of my securities licenses to learn how to do financial planning and wealth management. Along the way, I met some great people who encouraged me to get my Certified Financial Planning designation. The guidelines were changed after I started my studies, and I didn't get my certification. I was extremely disappointed.

During the 2008 recession, I lost my job at the bank. I had a non-compete at the time, so I used my securities licenses to explore the insurance industry. I was excited, and I thought it would be a career I could excel in. It turned out to be very challenging for me. I was learning and trying to sell at the same time. It was commission only, so I was always wondering where my next paycheck was going to come from. I drained my savings, learned a lesson, and was forced to go back into banking. After this experience, I encountered other managers who were very impressed by my accomplishments, but not willing to pay me for my experience, my skills, and the value I brought to the table. This was shortly after the recession and the salaries were still very low. At times, I felt that I was being discriminated against because I was Hispanic and had an accent. It is not true that people with accents are not very smart.

Life continued to throw curveballs at me, and I kept on fighting along the way. I went from one job to another trying to get the salary I deserved. By then, I was already in my forties and officially a middle-aged woman. Then I started asking myself some of the BIG questions. I wondered what the rest of my life was going to look like. What was my purpose here? Do I keep on working just to pay bills and then die? I felt depressed and miserable. By then, I was already in my fourth marriage with no more children. It was a good relationship for the most part. However, after ten years, I was starting to feel empty inside. Almost every weekend, I would go to the mall and spend money I didn't have and fill the void. By then, my daughter had gotten married, and I was dealing with the empty nest syndrome on top of that. In my search for something different, and something else to fill the void, I signed up for ballroom dance lessons. Then, I felt alive again! In the meantime and while literally having a ball, I created more debt for myself paying for the lessons, buying cute dresses, and dancing shoes.

Soon after this, I announced to my family that I was separating from my fourth husband. They were all devastated by the news and very sad for me. It never was my intention to actually go through another divorce again. I loved my husband, and we both agreed at the time that a separation would be healthy for us and help us get clear about things. I thought I would find my way back to him, but I never did, and I kept on searching for something more.

This led me to an amazing woman, Mary Morrissey, who later became my mentor and teacher. She was a former Science of Mind Minister who provided me with a new way of understanding and interpreting my faith and spirituality. I attended many retreats with her and other amazing women who were also asking the same big questions. These retreats would fill my heart with joy and peace and make me feel grounded. I also started reading books that would expand my curiosity about the meaning of life. Then, on one very special weekend in Sedona, Arizona, while attending one of her retreats, I made the decision that I wanted to be a spiritual life coach and create the same blissful experience for other women. I talked to Mary, my mentor, and she asked me many questions and encouraged me to sign up for her program. A year later, I got my certification. Excited to lead retreats and take women on amazing trips, I started my coaching business while still working at the bank. It was a side hustle for me, and my heart was on fire and ready to build a new dream!

The same year, on my 50th birthday, my new boyfriend proposed to me. At the time, it all seemed so perfect, and this time it was going to be forever. My soul mate had finally arrived! Actually, not so fast, it actually derailed me again. Without even realizing what I was doing, I put my dream and coaching materials away and began to make my new wedding plans. I spent endless hours planning every little detail. I was sure this was going to be my last wedding, so I wanted everything to be perfect.

I remember having my vision board with the ring, the ocean ceremony, and even my new home with the red door. Literally everything on that vision board manifested for me like magic! I couldn't believe it. Nine months later, the fairytale ended, and we got divorced. I felt so betrayed. My whole world came crashing down on me again. It felt like the dark night of my soul. I was devastated for months and went back into a depression. I remember keeping myself busy working two jobs, so I didn't have to deal with my new reality. Shortly after this setback, I filed for bankruptcy and started over. It was the best decision for me at the time in spite of the guilt and the shame that surrounded me.

My spirituality was my saving grace. The birth of my sweet granddaughter, Olivia, was also a blessing. She gave me purpose again, and a new reason to be strong and continue to move forward. She is my WHY and the reason I stay open to new possibilities. Now, I am creating a legacy for her and my daughter. I have big dreams!

As a Hispanic woman who could barely speak English, I have endured the good, the bad, and the ugly, and made it through thus far. All of the setbacks and endless hours of despair have taught me many lessons. It is like stepping stones along the path, and I continue to learn more every day. I look at life in a new way and a different light. I am stronger and wiser, and my soul has expanded greatly. I am constantly investing in my personal growth and development. I continue to read amazing books and follow great teachers and mentors. I surround myself with people that are successful and wiser so that I can learn from them. We all have access to infinite tools and resources on the Internet, and I have taken advantage of this.

I am aware and recognize what matters most, and I'm grateful for all the blessings in my life. I know that every day is a gift. When I lie on my pillow at night, I give thanks that I made it through another day. I know that tomorrow is not promised. God simply provided me with the lessons and the material I needed to teach others. As a spiritual life coach, my assignment now is to empower and support other women who are experiencing a divorce, are standing on the edge of one, or have made it to the other side of this painful time. I want to help them walk through this journey and make a difference in their lives. I want to connect them to the invisible side of success!

I was born under the sign of Leo, and the sun is my ruler. I need to continue to rise and shine every morning! I was born to lead others and be creative. I am a fun, loving, and nurturing woman who wants to see others succeed. I am also strong, a little stubborn, and very resilient. I have learned to love many things, continue to be optimistic about the future, and stay open to the possibilities. I count my blessings every day. My spiritual path has allowed me to understand the meaning of discernment as I continue to search for the meaning of this thing called life. There is always something greater, and the possibilities are endless. Self-mastery is a journey, not a destination.

# Charlotte Shaff

**Founder of The Media Push**

*H*eart Word: Stay Positive / Dealing with the emotional roller coaster of cancer can bring a person down a lot. Staying positive has helped me see beyond the fog and kept me going.

Charlotte Shaff grew up watching her parents own and manage a small business in Michigan and helped them with promotional ideas as a young teen. Her desire to help get the word out and promote for others blossomed when she studied Broadcasting and Advertising at Central Michigan University. She has a long history in customer service and a professional background that ranges from promotion, producing, and writing for TV news, community and seasonal media relations for Fiesta Bowl and MCDOT, to promotional and added value support for Subway restaurants.

Using these diverse experiences, she now helps local small business owners gain traditional and social media attention as experts in their industries. She is a WAHM (work at home mom), a former main contributor to a top local PR blog, and speaks routinely on the benefits of PR and social media as an integral way to learn, share, and educate others.

# *The C Word*

## By Charlotte Shaff

Bunches, Love you!!! XOXO (John)

These are the words that appeared on a yellow sticky note attached to multiple doctors' orders to schedule a mammogram. My husband, a physician assistant, was nagging me about what I needed to do to keep my health up (including getting that mammogram). But I wasn't listening—until I saw that yellow sticky note.

Each year I received a new order from my doctor for a mammogram, and I just kept filing them away in my home office. When my husband was pulling something out of the filing cabinet, he saw all the unfulfilled orders for mammograms from the past four years. He asked, "You haven't gotten a mammogram yet?" I said, "No, I don't have any breast cancer in my family. Every time I go to my doctor, nobody sees anything in my blood or feels anything in my breast." He said, "Charlotte, you're in your mid-40s. A doctor gives you orders for a reason." I was like, "Okay, whatever." A couple weeks later, he pulled out the doctor's orders and attached that little sticky note telling me he loved me.

My first instinct was to prove his worries wrong. So, I scheduled my mammogram in early March 2018. After leaving my appointment, they called me about an hour later and said, "We see some things that we think you need to come back for." I was floored.

**You need to take care of yourself because nobody else is going to do it for you.**

As they didn't seem to be too urgent about it, I wasn't afraid. It was just before we left for a spring break trip so I pretty much forgot all about it until I came back. I went back for a biopsy and ultrasound in early April. As the tech performed the ultrasound, I said something about them never ending up being cancer. The tech looked at me and said, "I'd be surprised if it wasn't cancer." After I got off the table, I called my husband. First of all, they're not supposed to say that kind of stuff to you, and now I was alarmed. A few days later, I had an MRI.

I distinctively remember where I was when I got the call from my doctor. I was checking out at Target and I picked up the phone instead of letting it go to voicemail like I normally would. She said of the three biopsies, for sure two are cancerous. I was like, "Holy crap!" Usually, you only hear about one tumor. So, I had three. That's when we started looking around to create the best team possible for this journey I was about to embark on.

**Everybody needs an angel; mine is my husband and soul mate, John.**

I love sports, especially football, so when I started my own public relations firm, The Media Push, in 2005, I purchased three season tickets for the Arizona Cardinals with the idea of taking my clients and friends to the games. In this particular year, the Cardinals were having one of the worst seasons. Nobody was coming to the games. There was this handsome guy sitting right next to me that I hadn't noticed before in the third to the last game of the season. We started chatting. He said he attended every game, and I shared I did too. That's when he said, "I know, I've been sitting right here right next to you the whole time." In my defense, when I brought guests, I didn't pay too much attention to the people around me as I was focused on them. It turns out; I should have been more aware of my surroundings.

After this conversation with John, I was nervous about going to the next game and talking to him again. So, when I brought my friends, I sat two seats over from my regular seat. I didn't share why I was doing this with my friends. Meanwhile, my friend noticed this guy next to her, who kept turning toward her to look at me. John and I didn't talk to each other that time, but I couldn't get him off my mind.

The last game of the season was approaching. I knew this was my last shot to get to know John. Tailgating before the game, I gathered some liquid courage as I shared my story with my two girlfriends and enlisted their help in doing some detective work for me. We were on a mission. By the end of the game, we would know, among other details, his age, occupation, and whether he was single or not. When I arrived at my seat, he was already sitting down in his seat. We started chatting and hit it off. By the end of the game, we took out our Blackberrys and shared email addresses. The result? More on that later.

**I had to make some tough decisions.**

With my newfound diagnosis of breast cancer, I had to make some tough decisions. Many people suggested I needed a mastectomy to remove that one breast. However, a lot of women that I talked to said they wished they had a bilateral mastectomy because the cancer either came back later or they live their life in fear each day that it's going to come back into their other breast. So, I did an "Angelina Jolie" and had a bilateral mastectomy, reconstruction, and then a hysterectomy. And I'm convinced I did the right thing as after my mastectomy, the doctor said there were actually five tumors, not three. As the cancer had not spread to my lymph nodes, and my Oncotype scores were low, I just had radiation treatments but no chemo.

While my husband appeared strong on the outside, I knew he was very worried on the inside because his medical mind goes to all the bad things that could happen. When my husband was 19 years old, he had a brain tumor which influenced his career path in medicine. He recognized the people who really took the time to care for him when he was sick. And he was there for me every step of the way.

During this time, I needed support, and I found it by posting my journey on social media. When I received my results that I had breast cancer, I posted a photo of that sticky note my husband wrote on top of the doctor's orders for a mammogram. I shared it on social media not because I wanted sympathy, but more as a public service announcement. I never thought it would happen to me. What if I never got a mammogram? What could have happened to me if I ignored all the signs?

**When a doctor gives you orders to get something done, you need to get it done.**

After the surgery, my doctor needed to determine my treatment plan. It was a very stressful time, as I wasn't sure if I needed chemo or not. Was I going to lose my hair? You might find this silly, but during high school, I was voted as having the best hair. So, part of me was scared that I was going to have to lose all my hair. As someone who has been recognized for great hair, losing it felt devastating at the time. When I received the news, I posted on social media and in my private breast cancer group, how excited I was to keep my hair. My husband shot a photo of me when I left the doctor's office of me, shaking my hair around. In the post, I shared I wasn't going to lose my hair, I didn't need chemo, and I was so excited about it. In the breast cancer private group, I had people say, "How dare you share this news when people are dealing with the trauma and agony of losing their hair! How dare you." People were private messaging me to take down the post.

I would never intend to be mean or hurt people devastated by the loss of their hair. I thought I was in this breast cancer group to share both highs and lows. As I waited much longer than most people to find out if I needed chemo, I felt like I wanted to share this good news. Most people go off to chemo as soon as their doctor gives them the thumbs up. This wasn't my situation. I waited while my doctor went on a vacation in Europe before receiving the news I wouldn't need chemo. It was more than a month to get that news. In the private group, I was told it was not okay to share this news. So, I took myself out of that group and I felt ashamed for what I did. I stopped posting for a bit and put a disclaimer on my social media posts stating, "I'm in no way trying to shame people who have lost their hair and people who have gone through cancer." Basically, I was just sharing my story.

**I learned a valuable lesson here.**

I will be more careful on what I post in these types of groups as I feel like sometimes people go there because they're scared. And the only emotion they know and understand is the anger, and the negativity. In my experience and in my opinion, they may feel more comfort being negative than they do by being positive. Some of those groups appeared to feed people's negativity and anguish as they shared their horrible experiences. Throughout my cancer journey, I shared on Facebook and Instagram just small victories and day brighteners like when my girlfriend came over and washed my hair and blew it out. On my posts, I wanted to show people what it was like to be on this cancer journey. I refuse to be that person who wants people to feel sorry for me. I don't want people to feel pity for me because that's just going to bring me down, too. I believe in the amazing power and influence of social media for the GOOD in this world and was an early adaptor of

Twitter and Instagram. As a work at home mom, I craved that social aspect.

Today, I look at what I've shared on social media as being kind of a public service announcement. I continue to get messages from friends and followers letting me know they got a mammogram, and they were thinking of me the whole time. For me, finding a positive support group was super important.

Some people don't want to tell people about it because they're scared. They don't want people to feel bad for them. They shouldn't feel scared. Instead, they'll become stronger by being able to share this journey because in some circles, the cancer is still considered the C word.

**A cancer diagnosis has a way of changing and impacting relationships.**

My sons knew something was going on because I was going to a lot more doctors' appointments. We decided not to share anything with them about my diagnosis until I had my surgery date because my young sons were sweet, sensitive boys (ages six and eight) and had a tendency to take on other people's emotions. As the surgery date approached, my husband shared with the boys, "I want you guys to know that mommy has got to go to the hospital, but everything's gonna be okay. Do you remember when you were younger, and you had ear infections all the time, and we took you to the doctor to get your tonsils and adenoids out? Do you remember after that, you didn't get sick as much? And remember I had something bad in my head. So, the doctors took it out, and now I'm better. Well, mommy has got something that's making her sick in her breast. So, the doctor's going to take the bad stuff out so she can feel better." The boys just nodded their heads and said, "Okay."

Looking back, I was raised in an environment where we didn't freak out about things. I was born and raised in a small farm town, Riga, in southeast Michigan. The town is so small the only traffic light is a caution light. My parents had a tree nursery and landscaping business, and I grew up on a farm surrounded by corn and soybeans. I went to college at Central Michigan University and majored in broadcasting and advertising with a dream of working in television. I worked in TV in Grand Rapids, Michigan, and lived there for five years. During this time, I worked on improving my skills in producing, writing, and editing. I loved it except for the cold. So, I sent my resume tapes to all the cities that were warm and ended up in Phoenix, Arizona, back in 1999. After working in the television industry for three years as a promotion producer and writer, and then in a variety of communications and advertising jobs, I formed my own public relations firm in 2005 where I worked from home, which eventually allowed me to be active in my sons' lives.

**I never really cried until June 6th, my surgery date, when they injected this blue dye into my veins.**

I broke down realizing what I was about to endure. For the first time, I realized the severity of the situation and how when I woke up, things were going to be different. That's the only time I cried. My parents came out for my surgery. It felt comforting having my mother, who is a former registered nurse, at my side. She assured me everything would be okay. During my healing journey, my mom took the boys to camp every day and helped with meals and cleaning. Another friend started a meal train for us.

In November of 2018, I had a hysterectomy where I had my uterus and ovaries, my "girl parts," taken out. For breast cancer survivors, many times the cancer comes back in those areas of the body. Since I knew I wasn't going to have any more kids, I opted to get it all taken out. On social media, I shared what it was like to have these scars and a body stripped of hormones. Today, I take antidepressants, have mood swings, hot flashes, and experience brain fogs. My joints are sore, and I feel like an 80-year-old lady when I get out of bed each morning. I need to exercise and eat better. It is a serious life-changer to endure cancer. It changes you to the core.

What I've learned on this journey is that the more open I've been, the more positive I've become about my prognosis and future. I know people are rooting for me, and I feel their positivity, which helps me get through this.

**Finding that positivity is key.**

There's a great group of breast cancer doctors in Phoenix. My physician was amazing, and my plastic surgeon who my doctor referred to as "Doctor Hollywood" really is a rock star surgeon. He performed my reconstruction during my bilateral mastectomy. Due to the radiation treatments, my right breast got a bit hard, and I had a hard time lifting my arm up. In August 2019, I had surgery to replace my implants and take out the hardened tissue matter and capsule. My breasts look great, though I have no nipples. I jokingly tell people that I look like a Frankenstein Barbie.

I have shared my journey from the start, and received so much support because of it. This is the time that you want people to encourage and help you. It's amazing the support you get and what you can give back. A former TV producer and friend of mine reached out to me because she found out she had breast cancer.

Even though she's not on social media a lot, when she told some friends about her diagnosis, they all said, "Charlotte had breast cancer, you need to reach out to her." So, she did. The first thing she said was, "I need to know everything. I'm scared. I don't know what to do." As a result of this connection, I talked her through everything happening with me. I gave her advice on what she needed to know before she went to the hospital, including what kind of support she would need after. I believe she felt so much better and relieved after our conversation. Once she scheduled her surgery, she was able to share more openly about her diagnosis with friends. Girlfriends threw her a "tatas" party prior to her surgery to support her and provide encouragement. She connected with friends she hadn't seen in years. She would have missed out on all that love and support if she didn't have the courage to share. Today, she has an amazing support group that will always be at her side. We continue to meet up every month to talk about our experiences in this journey.

My breast cancer diagnosis has not only been a wake-up call for me, but a public service announcement to my friends and family. For many of us, when we think of the word cancer, we immediately picture a frail, dying bald woman hooked up to chemo. That woman was not me. And social media was going to help me share my story in an honest way.

With social media today, often people put their best face forward, and we all know that everybody has things going on. That's why I'm sharing my cancer journey in such a raw way. I want people to know when you get cancer; it's not a death sentence. You don't know what your treatment will be as you may not need chemo, or even radiation. You don't know. I'm an advocate of taking control of your life and your health.

**Getting back to that last Arizona Cardinals game of the season.**

John and I sharing our contact information via our Blackberrys was a win/win even though the Cardinals sucked that season. Shortly after, John asked me out for dinner (our first date was January 4th, 2007) and we've been together ever since. Plus, we still have the same season tickets. The Arizona Cardinals brought us together. They say you'll find that special someone in a place you'd never expect. And there he was, my soul mate, sitting right next to me at the Cardinals game.

# *Veronica Bahn*

**Founder and CEO of Side Hustle Expert LLC./ Financial Freedom Entrepreneur/ wife/ mom/ friend/ baseball mom/ speaker/ author/ Reiki certified/ business coach**

*H*eart Word: Humility / At its very root it means being teachable and coachable. It means living life in a way where learning, growing, and expanding helps us to become our very best. This word is the hub of my world. All things flow for me from a space of humility. The Latin translation is "humus" meaning soil. Nutrient-dense fortified soil where a seed planted can transform, and where the roots can grow and become strong. It means being willing to accept change so that we can change the world knowing our life's trials created the humus in which we can prosper and succeed.

Veronica Bahn is an attraction marketer, entrepreneur, mom boss, sales expert, author, and speaker. Her work inspires collaborative connections with like-minded people who desire a world that expands in abundance, success, and kindness.

Veronica is a leader in her industry and has earned many awards in her tenure with NuSkin. With hard work and dedication, she replaced her full-time income and as an Ambassador for Nourish the Children, she and her collaborative partners proudly feed nearly a thousand meals each month to children throughout the world. Her unique ability to bring empathy, energy to the people she has transformed through coaching creates an empowering formula for success.

Veronica's newest business venture is the creation of Side Hustle Expert, LLC. She assists high-achieving women by turning their passion into profits. By developing a strategy to generate thousands of dollars in extra income every month, her clients are redefining their side hustle story. Through her own personal experience and success, her programs offer tools and techniques through online group and one-on-one development coaching, a free downloadable guide to identify your passion project and her remote Reiki sessions to clear the stress and anxiety around building a work-from-home business.

Family time is a treasure, whether it's alone time with her supportive husband of 31 years, beach time, tennis, pickleball, reading, or dancing in the kitchen while making dinner, nothing is more important than how she creates the life she loves with her family.

What's stopping you from creating the life you love? What if your side hustle success story is one small shift away from becoming a reality and nurturing generations of lives? Now is the time.

Veronica believes "It's time to cultivate a magical grid of peace, love, abundance, and light that will flow freely around the planet and lift others to their highest vision of victory. Every day it begins with me."

# What Happens to a Dream Deferred?

## By Veronica Bahn

We all have dreams, and is there anything more innocent and pure than a dream of an 8-year-old? My niece set up a lemonade stand to earn some extra money and donate a portion of her proceeds to charity. Her generous and entrepreneurial spirit moved me. How could someone so young already be turning lemons into lemonade? I believe in signs, and I remember this Saturday morning so vividly because six weeks later, I was selected to share my story in this book.

As I drank my lemonade, I began to reflect on how far my husband and three children had come in the last 11 years, how we rebuilt our dreams out of unexpected lemons. So much has changed in those years. As I reflect, I take in the sunset on the balcony of our new dream home. This home has not only afforded me the views and sunsets of my dreams, but my husband and I started creating the vision as we were in the depths of despair and depression in the summer of 2008.

Our new home represents the end of our rebirth as we grew and learned how to dream again. I never thought we would face the type of lemons we were handed. I am overwhelmed with emotion from all the trials, tender mercies, and manifestations we have experienced and overcome as a family. But we did it! We took a leap with faith and trusted our journey.

The lemonade we carefully, dutifully made as we rebuilt our lives ended up being more delicious and satisfying than anything we could have dreamed of. It took falling apart in order to find myself.

I will never forget the summer of July 2008. We were on a dream vacation in Sun River, Oregon, with our children and family friends, who happen to be my husband's business partner. At Sun River, there are endless adventures in the great outdoors. There are rivers flowing with rafters and kayakers, and miles of trails for walking, biking, and horseback riding. I can still smell the marshmallows roasting in the evenings mixed with the aroma of pine trees. I still vividly recall the night sky with the endless sea of stars mixed in with the deep dark depths of space displaying the most amazing constellations. All of us found ourselves just soaking it all in—it was a magical place—a magical place for new beginnings we never saw coming.

On day four of our incredible eight-day adventure, we went river rafting. This was something we had never done before. It was thrilling to feel the raft plunge through the rapids and witness the water soaking us from head to toe—it was an adrenaline rush! I'll never forget when they taught us how to get back in the raft. To get out of the rough water, you have to go against every instinct. You need to submerge yourself in the water before being brought back up for air. The guides had to use that momentum of pushing you deeper into the water to propel you out of it.

That evening, we sat on our porch with our friends planning the next day's adventure. We then talked about what the next few years would look like for all of us. We began making a wish list of places we wanted to go in the upcoming years. We were fortunate that our careers were on track. Retirement looked possible within the next seven years. We had been blessed with the growth of our business, and we were living our dreams. Our 20th anniversary was two months away, and we were planning on celebrating in Italy. The family was healthy and happy. Our home was filled with joy. The great recession hadn't reached us yet.

Thankfully, my husband and I have always known how volatile our industry can be. Having a career in sales means that income fluctuates. We kept six months of savings in our rainy day fund. It wasn't always easy doing this, especially when times were good—it's hard to see the dark coming when you're surrounded by light. The phone call we never anticipated came that evening we had spent looking at fireflies and constellations with our kids. That phone call upturned our lives, and we joined the company of millions of other Americans during an economic recession. After giving 17 years of our lives to a company, Chuck and I were no longer part of the new plan.

No one plans to be abruptly downsized and outsized from their business. And for us, we lost our dual-income overnight. We were independently commissioned sales reps working together side-by-side in a business that we loved and were very good at. We were a team. The formula worked great for us. It's really all we ever knew. We took pride in our customer service and the relationships we built over time. We had a great work-life balance and loved that we could work from home and be there for our children when they needed us. It was a win-win.

What do you do when you are angry and confused and fearful of what is next? I did what I do best. I grabbed my husband and held him. I told him it would be okay even though I wasn't sure yet how. I wanted to scream into the night. I wanted to pick up the phone and call the man who made that decision. I wanted to give him a piece of my mind. What kind of person does that? Who calls two dedicated, loyal employees of 17 years on their family vacation and tells them they were no longer needed?

We had four days left with our kids and dear friends before we were scheduled to go back home. Looking back, thank goodness for those friends and how they embraced us at that moment. The distraction of still being on our trip with activities planned and kids to laugh with was a godsend. Even though it was a very difficult few days, I can now see how God's plan was beginning to unfold. I held onto the anger for far too long at the people who made that decision. It was dark and heavy time—not unlike learning how to get back in the raft. We had to be plunged under, into cold darkness, not knowing which way was up—until a helpful hand grabbed us and pulled us to safety.

Reality hit hard when the trip was over, and the kids were back to school. How do you prepare for a future job when you can hardly get out of bed? How do you put your best foot forward when fear takes over, and the weight of the world feels like it is on your shoulders? How do you convince yourself to breathe through this difficulty when every breath hurts? How do you wake up with a smile on your face to get your kids off to school, knowing your future is so uncertain? How do you dream when your only thought is finding your next paycheck? How in the world does inspiration and trust flow through you when your belief and hope is at an all-time low?

**The answer I found was: love, faith, and humility.**

We would do whatever was necessary to lift each other up daily. Slowly through our devotion and dedication to each other, Chuck and I were able to hope again. There is no greater power than in a hug. We gave hugs freely and as often as necessary, not just to each other, but to family and friends who had our backs. It gave us comfort at a time when we needed it.

Having long-lasting relationships cultivates a culture of close friendships. These are the kinds of friends you can count on during the hard times. Even though we cancelled our anniversary trip to Italy, we promised each other that within ten years we would get there. Knowing our deep disappointment in not going to Italy, to our surprise, our sweet daughter, Lexy, created an Italian night to remember. Our lifelong friends hosted the event, and the celebration was priceless. I believe that single thoughtful moment was a catalyst to waking ourselves up. The fact that our daughter and friends recognized how much we needed a party like this to celebrate this day still takes my breath away. Friends we now call family were there to help pull us to safety.

As we began to search for new careers—I became the CHO (Chief Home Officer). I was the expert in trimming the fat off our monthly budget. Without any income, I had to figure out a way to reduce our expenses by one-third. We all quickly learned the difference between a need and a want. If it wasn't necessary to survive, it was gone. Cutting coupons became a weekly activity for the kids and me. We looked to our safety net of friends for job referrals.

It was time to start turning lemons into lemonade. Six months went by, and Chuck landed on his feet. I will never forget the phone call that made this happen. I dropped to my knees and sobbed. All the pain and anger I was feeling suddenly came flowing out of me. Everything I had pent up released at that moment. With a grateful heart, I went to my journal and wrote, "It's my turn now." Chuck and I decided multiple streams of income was a better idea. This time we would not put all our eggs in one basket.

With Chuck employed, my goal was to find a new career that would provide us with the health insurance we needed and the stability of a paycheck, while his job was still sales-dependent. I had my degree and years of experience to fall back on but, what I did not count on was all those years I was working from home actually hindered my prospects. In my role supporting my husband, I lacked the face-to-face time and the industry experience they were looking for. I was also competing with a flood of people in the same situation as me.

The year 2008 was the most emotional year of my life. It was full of stress, sacrifice, fear, and anxiety. At 42-years-old, I hardly recognized myself. I had aged and was sad and depressed. As I looked in the mirror, reality struck. I needed to take 100 percent responsibility for where I was. If things were going to change, I needed to change. I was facing an uphill climb. I did not receive a paycheck by placing second place in job interview after job interview.

I began the process of change by writing down what I wanted to accomplish and what brought me joy. I began to examine how I showed up in the world, what I wanted to do, who I wanted to do it with, where I wanted to do it, when I wanted to do it, and how I wanted to do it.

Even though my job situation wasn't changing, I was beginning to let myself dream again. We had come out of the darkest days together as a family.

I believed in myself and my abilities. I was willing to do whatever it took to get the job done. I knew the answer started with asking the right question. I needed to create my own dream job. I realized that my journey with my faith and relationship with God had taken a back seat. When things are going well, it doesn't seem as necessary to pray and give thanks. Reconnecting to my faith inspired me to keep going. It renewed my sense of understanding that God is always there, even when we're not turning to him for help and guidance.

Despite my renewed faith and understanding, failing at achieving what I desire was new to me. No matter how much work I was doing on myself, I couldn't manifest the right opportunity for my family and me. This was unfamiliar territory. Self-sabotaging attacks were common as I told myself, "This wouldn't have happened if you were focused on your faith, if you prayed more, if you went to church more, or if you were more grateful for what you had." This personal tongue lashing lasted for about a year. But honestly, I hid it well. I knew I had so much to work through. It became a time of spiritual discovery which included daily prayer, writing in my gratitude journal, reading personal development books, and confiding in good people that lifted me up. It was going to be the only way to shift out of my depression, feeling of loss, and not knowing what I was worthy to do next.

I am a firm believer in the power of three especially since I was looking for signs showing me what to do every day. Finally, in August of 2009, that began to happen. At this point, Chuck had been working for his new company for about six months. He even added new accounts to his roster. I find it fascinating that when your life is in momentum, exciting opportunities continually appear. My job at home continued to be cutting coupons and expenses. I handled all our investments and retirement stocks. I partnered with my cousin, who had years of experience and hired him to help us navigate through the 2008 Wall Street debacle. Daily, I searched for growing companies in North America while I was job hunting during this recession.

The first message came from a gal who approached me at a weekend event I was working at with Chuck. She first told me I was beautiful and had beautiful skin. I immediately thought, "What are you selling?" She asked if I heard about this anti-aging company, and she thought I would be a great representative. Quite honestly, I did know this company and was actually surprised to learn that they were still in business. Initially, I learned about them in 1988 and was not interested in pursuing a business partnership with them at that time. But, somehow this angel appeared to me out of nowhere and shared that their stock was $9.00 in April of 2009, and now it was $19.00. I was fascinated by this information and looked the company up on Monday. Sure enough, they were a publicly traded company trending up because of a new skincare technology that was on fire across the globe. So, what did I do? I bought the stock, of course.

In August 2009, my daughter, Lexy, was heading to college on a full-ride honors journalism scholarship. My son, CJ, was headed into his sophomore year of high school, and baseball was his life. My son, Erick, was still in elementary school loving life and his dog Ritz. The kids were thriving amidst the adjustments that came with their parents being unemployed. It's amazing how much money you can save when you eat at home, cut expenses, and have a daughter receiving a full-ride college scholarship. In that year, I learned more from my kids than they did from their mom.

When we moved Lexy to campus that fall, this mama's heart was experiencing a void. Watching her go was like watching a vacuum continually sucking the energy out of our house and air out of my chest. Inside I was still really struggling. I kept asking myself, "Did I spend enough time with her? Is she prepared? Was I present enough with everything going on? Does she know how much she is loved and how talented and smart she is?" That day as we waved goodbye, my second sign appeared, I vowed that I was going to find a career and have a passion she could look up to. I wanted my journey to somehow give her unwavering strength and a positive voice as she began her adult life.

A few months later, my cell phone rang from a number I didn't recognize. I was shocked to hear a familiar voice say, "Hello." It had been about 25 years since I heard from my beautiful friend, Becky. She had no idea what Chuck and I had gone through in the last year or that I was not working. I was so happy to hear from her that I never even asked her what she was doing. We planned to connect the following week.

Becky and Shauna showed up at my door. As they stood in front of me, I noticed my darling friends from high school came bearing gifts of food, fellowship, a business plan, and an outstretched hand. As I welcomed them into my home, I caught a glimpse of a logo—it was the same company I just bought stock in three weeks prior. There it was standing right in front of me, my third sign. I looked up to the heavens and smiled. Little did my friends realize, I was all in on this business opportunity that Monday, October 26th, 2009.

Talk about taking a leap of faith! I decided to partner with this company as it would be the vehicle to help me create my business from home. I invested in my new business, plopped down my credit card, and three days later, my starter kit arrived. I wasted no time in getting started. My business took off, and I recouped my investment in two weeks. I was ready to give this my all!

The one thing I didn't anticipate with jumping straight into this new venture—I was gone all the time. In addition to working his new job, Chuck was now picking up the slack from all the household chores and daily home operations that I had been doing for a year. It became apparent I needed to make some shifts and changes because now my family life was suffering. I needed to discover how to balance everything. I needed a plan—a road map to success. I also discovered I was not very coachable and taking advice was something I needed to work on. I thought with my previous business success, advanced education, and achieving every goal and plan I had put out there to accomplish, was going to be enough. I believed I was fully prepared for this new entrepreneurial venture.

I needed to go back to where I started this journey. My family was on solid ground. Chuck was thriving with his new accounts. I had found something I was great at! I began writing down what I wanted to accomplish in this business and what brought me joy. I am a reader. I believe leaders are readers and learners are earners. I decided to start my day with personal development. I began to read books like Jack Canfield's Success Principals, Og Mandino's The Greatest Secret in the World, and Napoleon Hill's Think and Grow Rich.

I needed to take what I learned working with my husband, and the 20 years I had been running our household. Once I began to understand that working from home in this new space just needed a plan and a vision—my business and family life got back on track.

Fast forward to today. I'm celebrating my ten-year anniversary with the same company. The company that found me in my darkness has created a light for myself and my family. It has provided for us. It has afforded me possibilities I never thought possible. It has taken my family around the world from South Africa to Belize to Alaska. It allowed my husband and I to take that dream vacation to Italy. Most of all, I found myself.

I am convinced our year of challenge brought my family closer and led us to where we are today. We support each other through our successes and failures because we do it together. We challenge ourselves every day to connect with others, show up, recognize abundance, and have a win-win mentality as we serve others. Chuck is still thriving in sales with retirement on the horizon. Lexy graduated from college, is working in social media in Los Angeles, and is about to get married. My son, CJ, has worked through baseball-related injuries and is now finishing his business degree. He has a personal coaching business and is the pitching coach for Benedictine University. My youngest son, Erick, followed his brother's footsteps and is studying business and playing college baseball at Benedictine University.

Without this journey through hardship, I don't know if I ever would have realized my full potential. I am a proud wife, mother, daughter, and sister, but I am also an entrepreneur, a business owner, a mentor, a leader, an author, and a motivational speaker. I champion causes for women and children. It is this entrepreneurial spirit that made me so eager to contribute to my niece's lemonade stand. I hope to inspire women I meet all over the world. I know firsthand how hard it is to turn lemons into lemonade. My secret recipe is to add an extra dose of love, faith, and humility.

# Vickie Mudra

### CEO and Founder of the Institute for Deliberate Practice

*H*eart Word: Courage is a Choice is my truth / After almost 50 years of overcoming trauma and tragedy in my life, I one day recalled hearing my mother repeatedly offer the same advice, "You have a choice." While it had slight variations over the years, the message was the same—we can choose the meaning for each experience in our life. We can choose to be a victim of our circumstances or we can rise up and lean into our courage. Courage is a choice that can never be taken away. Choose Courage.

Vickie Mudra is a published author and speaker, as well as researcher, leadership development coach, and experiential learning expert. Curious to the core, Vickie invites her community to always ask themselves, "What if it could be different?" and helps them discover their courage to make the tough choices. Vickie knows that living in your purpose, deliberately—on purpose, is the most crucial thing we can do as part of this human experience.

She is widely recognized by executives, colleagues, and her clients for her deep talents in strategic impact and organizational effectiveness, quality improvement, and workforce development. She believes everyone deserves happiness and joy in their lives and suggests that increasing joy and connection in the workplace is the only way to win in the marketplace.

Vickie has over 30 years' experience in various industry sectors, including healthcare and non-profit organizational leadership. She received her BA in Healthcare Administration from DePaul University and has a Master's in Public Health from Benedictine University. She also holds graduate certification in Disaster Management, is Certified Six Sigma Lean in Healthcare, and is an ICF-ACC credentialed coach.

Today she is the CEO and founder of the Institute for Deliberate Practice, Inc. As a lifelong horse lover, Vickie supports the advancement of scientific evidence supporting the healing and growth that can occur between horses and humans, as well as increases in happiness and whole-being health. She will be adding equine-assisted learning and equine coaching to her program offerings in the future.

# Courage and Connection Is Our Strategy—Joy Is Our Weapon

## By Vickie Mudra

### The Secret to a Happy Life

~ NATIVE AMERICAN PARABLE

One day the Creator gathered all the animals and said:

'I want to hide the secret to a happy life from humans until they are ready for it.'

'Give it to me. I'll fly it to the moon,' said the Eagle.

'No, one day soon they will go there and find it.'

'How about the bottom of the ocean?' asked the Salmon.

'No, they will find it there too.'

'I will bury it in the great plains,' said the Buffalo.

'They will soon dig and find it there.'

'Put it inside them,' said the wise grandmother Mole.

'Yes,' said the Creator, 'it is the last place they will look.'

## We Have a Choice

I was standing on the front lawn. A few neighbors were standing around us, part of me relieved that my family didn't have to witness this alone, while another part was wondering what else these people could be doing on a Sunday morning besides watching my house burn down.

So many memories of that warm, sunny spring day in northern Illinois in May, just two months before I would turn 18 and just one month before high school graduation. I got up early that morning to go to work. I said goodbye to my parents and younger sisters, and drove off. They were still getting ready to leave for church. I remember glancing over to the birdcage where our family bird was cleaning his feathers before I closed the door behind me.

Only a couple hours had passed since then. Now, I found myself standing in shock, suddenly realizing that our bird was dead when a fireman threw my white prom dress over the second-story balcony and onto the front lawn. That was supposed to be my wedding dress. I was engaged to be married to my high school sweetheart, an event that took place 18 days after my 18th birthday. And to answer the question that may be floating around in your mind–I wasn't pregnant. There were many other good reasons we decided to get married at our tender, young ages. That's another story.

So many questions were racing through my mind. How did the fire start? What was salvageable? Why was my mom still at home but not my stepfather and sisters? Where would we live?

I don't remember crying … maybe I did. I do remember being frozen at the scene and hearing my mom say four words that I had heard before and would hear again: "We have a choice."

## What's in Your Backpack?

I believe when we're born, we are all issued an invisible bag. Sometimes I picture this bag like a sack that Santa uses to deliver toys (yes, I still believe, in case you're wondering). Other times I think it's more like a backpack that you wear around every day like it's part of your body.

From the moment we come into this world, things get put into our bag/backpack. These include lies that we were supposed to believe to be truth, cruel things said to us by family or friends on the playground, and the abusive and hurtful things that are done to us. Many times, things are added to our bags without our knowing or granting permission. Some things we actually put in there because we somehow found ourselves holding something and didn't know what else to do with it, so we just stuffed it into our bag. All these things can begin to weigh us down as we journey through life. The heavy burden of our gremlins–those fears, self-doubts, wounds, scars, and worries become heavier and heavier. The extra weight of our assumptions and limiting beliefs make us sometimes wonder how we can get out of bed and move through our days.

Meanwhile, some of the beautiful things that come inherently with our bag get taken out. Things like our curiosity and natural joy are pushed to the bottom, thereby extinguishing our intuition and wonder. We replace our vulnerability and trust with a need to control everything and cynicism that prevents real connection. We have come to believe that life is hard. We determine our value by comparing our worth to the worth of others. We live in the past and daydream about the future to the extent that we miss the present ... and the gifts of being present.

## The Year That Changed Everything

I never realized how heavy my bag had gotten until I was approaching the wonderful age of 50. The idea that I was going to be a half-century old might be daunting to some. It actually was the least of my concerns at the time, however. My only daughter had just gotten married in the fall–a spectacular and beautiful event, but still stressful on many levels. My son was engaged and scheduled to be married a couple months after my birthday—again, an amazing blessing. However, with both of my children embarking on their own life journeys, I was thrown into the full effect of an empty nest and all it implied within the same year as I was turning the big 5-0.

The weddings and becoming another decade older were up there on the stress scale, but nothing I couldn't handle. After all, I had survived my first four decades of life, which were not all that easy.

Having a mother who had been married three times, moving more times in my life than I had fingers and toes to count, and experiencing both ends of the prosperity scale, I was resilient and strong. When I turned 13, I finally felt safe enough to tell my mother about the six years of abuse I had experienced starting when I was 6. She told me I had a choice: to let it define me and live as a victim of my circumstances or pick myself up by my bootstraps and rise above it as a stronger young woman. At the age of 13, I didn't really know what that meant but I complied. Whenever adversity struck our family, up to and including the fire, she reminded me of those same words … be a victim or make a choice not to. I would successfully survive many more situations over the next 37 years of my life by employing those words. This was my mom's way of teaching me resiliency and empowering me to be strong enough to bounce back.

In that same year when I was turning 50 and the kids were starting their lives with their new soul mates, I also had significant changes at work. My work wasn't just a job—it was my passion and my life. For my entire adult life, besides being a wife and mother, I had defined myself by my career. After spending several years dedicating my time, energy, and identity to a growing corporation where I had been the proverbial big fish in a small, but expanding pond, I found myself becoming a little fish in a huge pond. My immediate manager left to join another organization and my employer—who had essentially become like another spouse—was no longer the same, dependable priority that nurtured my ego, valued my opinions, and gave me the autonomy to which I had become accustomed. I was experiencing something I really didn't like–change.

## *Time to Wake Up*

There were new managers, new ideas, new rules, and this challenged who I was–or at least who I thought I was. I fought back. Not in the obvious, non-compliant, unacceptable or unprofessional way but still fiercely–on the inside, quietly, and subtly. As hard as I tried to accept the changes, I couldn't do it alone. Only with the help of an amazing executive coach and supportive Human Resources team, was I able to increase my self-awareness and remind myself of my mother's words: I have a choice.

I had the opportunity to do a lot of exploration work on a series of executive leadership retreats and take the time to invest in who I was and what I was made of. Through an awakening that I was more than my job, my title, and my resume, I explored my values, my true strengths, and I found my purpose. I then challenged myself to make a tough choice—live out my purpose exactly where I was planted. Bring my best to the job. I made a commitment to my manager, my team, and my colleagues that for as long as I was employed at this organization, they deserved to be served from the best I had to give. I didn't have to like the changes, but I decided to adapt and accept. That awakening began a journey that I had no idea would take me where it did.

Ten years prior, I thought I had experienced the greatest loss of my life. I received a call that my mother had died suddenly at her desk at work. I remember racing to her office and fighting off the police officer guarding her office door, which was closed. Her boss, who was a friend of our family, along with another coworker who had performed CPR and happened to be a friend of my son's, all stood gathered around, speechless. I don't recall the words I used but I remember clearly the resolve I had to get to my mother. Once the coroner had come, they opened the door and let me in. I laid down next to my mom on the floor and begged her to wake up. She was wearing the diamond earrings I had just bought her a month before for her 60th birthday. She had always dreamed of having diamond earrings.

Healing from the death of my mother took a long time. She was my best friend. I had supported her through three marriages, helped her raise my younger sisters, and enjoyed her as a devoted grandmother to my two children and their two cousins. How would I ever fill the void left by her passing? I went through pictures, read her journals, and hung on every word and phrase that were her signature lines … including the fact that yes, I had a choice. Picking myself up and moving forward was certainly a choice and some days were more difficult than others. As I was turning 50, I was also facing the 10th anniversary of her death. I had remained resilient and gotten stronger but still had a way to go.

> "Happiness is not a luxury,
> it is the purpose of our existence."
>
> ~ DALAI LAMA

## Time to Connect

My ultimate test would come in January of the year I was turning 50. My husband had fallen at work the summer before and even a couple of months later, at our daughter's wedding, I definitely noticed that he didn't walk with the same smooth, gazelle-like strides he was known for all of his life. His stature wasn't as straight and his muscles weren't as strong and supple as they had been for the 32 years we had been married. He was losing that swagger he had when we were dating back in high school when he played football, basketball, and still held a school record in track. We had been together for a total of 34 years at that point and he is still the only person I have ever lived with besides my parents. Something was wrong and we knew it. The night before Thanksgiving we had received some bad news and were instructed to get a second opinion. The January of my 50th birthday year we would get confirmation of the bad news—my husband, my love, my high school sweetheart, the father of my children, and my soul mate—had Amyotrophic Lateral Sclerosis, ALS, Lou Gehrig's disease.

ALS is a progressive neurodegenerative disease that affects nerve cells in the brain and the spinal cord. In ALS patients, because the motor neurons progressively degenerate and eventually die, they stop initiating and controlling muscle movement, causing complete paralysis and death, usually between 2-5 years after diagnosis. Because my husband had already been experiencing symptoms for almost two years, panic set in and there was no stress level that could describe where I found myself. In between one successful wedding and planning for the second, along with the massive changes taking place professionally, I crumbled. I found myself driving down the road and having to pull over to just breathe as I would start hyperventilating. I wondered how I would survive and questioned if I even wanted to once death came for the one who taught me unconditional love and pure acceptance. His only request of me was that I wouldn't try to navigate this journey on my own.

Through the gift of my work, family, and my executive coach, I heard my mother's wise words: "You have a choice." Her words kept ringing in my ears as I saw my husband remain strong and independent, not giving in to the disease and refusing to give up.

Thankfully, his progression was quite slow and we had time to prepare for his early retirement a year later.

I started looking at things that weighed me down–things I discovered were sitting in my "bag" and asking, "What if it could be different?" While I may have mastered the art of resiliency and demonstrated strength time after time, this wasn't about bouncing back. This was about finding the courage to walk into a situation that looked and felt like a burning building and not knowing if or how I might emerge. It became crystal clear that there was a difference between resiliency and courage. While I had one, I needed to find the other.

Intuitively I believe my mom was encouraging my courage all along. She was trying to tell me not just to get up and bounce back from adversity, but rise up in confidence and not be afraid or intimidated to face the fire, walk into the lion's den, and be proud of my battle scars. I came to a new level of appreciation for both resiliency AND courage and wear both like a badge of honor today. I learned to connect with and start to love myself and for the first time, truly reach out to connect with others in a real, meaningful way. Sharing the news about his diagnosis with others created new and enhanced existing relationships in ways my husband hadn't previously anticipated. Courage and connection would be our strategy.

## Time to Energize

I found myself pulling stuff out of my own bag, questioning my assumptions and beliefs about my career path and wondering what else I could do that would allow me to follow my passion and honor my values. I started getting really curious about what I might learn from this part of my journey. I guess there are still a whole lot of lessons life has to teach us, even at 50. Because I had derived so much personal and professional value from excellent coaching, I wanted to learn more and see if that might be an avenue for me to share my gifts in the future. I immersed myself into coach training, established my areas of expertise in business consulting, got certifications in Conversational Intelligence and Happiness Studies, among others. I knew my strategy needed to include a well-equipped toolbox to accompany both my husband and I on this journey. I felt I needed as much coaching as possible and figured my friends and family would, too.

We started to put plans in place. The kids were married and had all taken jobs in Arizona, so after my son's wedding, both of my newlywed children and their new spouses headed out to move from Illinois, across country, to start their new lives in the West. I knew I didn't want to travel this ALS journey without our family so we made the decision to sell our home and also move to Arizona, something we had talked about for retirement anyway. Mike needed to accept that he would be required to retire from his job with the electric company after almost 27 years. Recognizing there are no coincidences, after a year in a slow real estate market, our house sale closed just two days after his retirement. We were on the road to our new life. He was newly retired and I was still working a corporate gig and exploring and connecting with who I was and what I wanted out of life.

Quite pleased with the lessons I had applied in my own workplace and the importance I had placed on my professional relationships, I wondered if I might have an opportunity to help others who were facing changes in their lives–personally and/or professionally. I explored how the principles I developed might help other leaders and teams who didn't have a mom who constantly reminded them that, "they have a choice." During my last year as a corporate leader, working remotely from my home in the desert, I shared my ideas and coached my team and colleagues who were also struggling with the changes. Many of them found their agency, exercised their voice, and stepped into their choice. That meant re-engaging and increasing their own effectiveness in their current roles. I noticed I had helped some reignite their energy. As a result, they went for promotions or explored other areas of the company where they could provide their gifts and talents. There were a couple of people who left the organization as they discovered new opportunities. Another person even started her own successful consulting business.

Through a deep understanding of what really matters and what lights you up, we can establish goals for ourselves and determine our own destiny. Despite my husband's illness, we had so much to be grateful for. His joy and sense of humor, just like his unconditional love, inspired me to not give up and grieve prematurely, but consider my passion and my gifts. We set goals, some individually, and some as a couple. Together we could walk into the burning building. We could enter the arena–and we had found our weapon that would help us—joy.

> "Then he said to them, "Go your way, eat the fat
> and drink sweet wine and send portions to him for whom
> nothing is prepared; for this day is holy to
> our Lord; and do not be grieved, for the
> joy of the LORD is your strength."
>
> ~NEHEMIAH 8:10

One of my goals was to leave my employer and start my own company. By this time, I had achieved a level of peace and harmony. I felt that leaving wasn't about me moving away from something negative, but rather truly moving toward a new opportunity to serve other organizations and inspire workplaces to envision excellence with new energy and engagement. Almost two years after his diagnosis, we were in our new home and I was launching a new business. He was retired and living his purpose as he always had— as my #1 cheerleader, business partner, accountability buddy, and lover of life. We made things happen and recommitted to our marriage, our relationships, and our future. We know there are no guarantees so we stopped living like his diagnosis took away something we never actually had–a promise of tomorrow. It just serves as an acute reminder that all we have is today. The present. A gift.

"Happiness is the meaning and the purpose of life,
the whole aim and end of human existence."

~ARISTOTLE

## Time to Transform

Connecting with new friends, networking in the healthcare community, showing up in support groups—letting go of fears about dying, removing the assumptions, and limiting beliefs from our bags—has become our new norm. There continues to be days where the burden and unknowns of the disease are heavy. We practice gratitude. We grieve as he loses physical function and his body can't do what it once could. We cry, but we laugh more. We celebrate. We dance. We wake up every day focused on our strategy to choose courage and connect always and in all ways, with each other and with our family and friends. We find ways to energize and engage and keep our cups full. We don't worry about what we can't control. We live 100% by the Serenity Prayer.

God, grant me the serenity
to accept the things I cannot change,
Courage to change the things I can,
And wisdom to know the difference.

Happiness starts on the inside. Cliché but also true. As an educator, a coach, a consultant, and a community-builder, happiness is something I believe in. As a public health professional, simulation expert, and organizational leader, I have spent over 15 years in the education and clinical preparation of future healthcare professionals. I have seen tremendous outcomes when we deliberately practice clinical and psychomotor skills. I also have seen the professional costs and personal suffering when our workforces are burning out and leaders are not caring for their greatest asset—their talented professionals.

There is so much we can't change in our lives and in our work. In healthcare and many other professions, systems are often the cause of stress. Through collaboration and heart-centered conversations, organizations and teams can keep what works well, stop what doesn't, and be open to finding new ways to improve. Paying attention to culture and ensuring it is characterized by commitment, engagement, passion, pride, and community support and fellowship can have a huge impact on retention and overall stakeholder satisfaction and effectiveness. Having the courage to change what we can change—making the decisions that are within your control—can lead to the greatest potential for personal and workplace joy.

We need to teach people to recognize they have a bag and invite them to dig through it like an old box in a basement or gathering dust in a garage. I will support people as they learn to unpack their fears and self-doubts, invite them to challenge the value of their assumptions and limiting beliefs, and love them as they find safety in community and be their authentic self. I encourage people to ask what their life and work could be without judgement of themselves or others. I ignite service professionals and caregivers to live empowered. I believe that joy and success are not mutually exclusive. My mission is to inspire the possibility for joy, courage, and connection throughout the world. What if joy were your weapon of choice?

Even though my mother was never a fan of higher education, having never completed college herself, she was extremely proud of my academic achievements and encouraged me as I finished both my undergraduate and graduate degrees. What I know to be true is that in her eyes, it was character and key relational competencies that held more value than any diploma.

Some people label things like good communication, decision-making, teamwork, problem solving, strong work ethic, the ability to be a leader who others want to follow, and flexibility as soft skills. My mother taught me it is these things that matter most and they are anything but soft and fluffy. She recognized and instilled the importance of relationships above everything else. She modeled love, hope, and gratitude. She never let me forget that I had more choices than I could ever imagine. She inspired me to share that message with others.

I share below ten essential skills as self-affirmations based on the Deliberate CARE™ model to get your journey started:

Awaken ~ Connect ~ Energize ~ Transform

"I Decide to make a difference for myself and others."
"I Explore who I am and what I want."
"I Love who I am and what I do."
"I Imagine unlimited possibilities for myself and am a life-long learner."
"I Build excellence around what matters most."
"I Engage all areas of my life and seek energetic balance."
"I Release thoughts, feelings, and beliefs that no longer serve me."

"I Am Authentic, appreciating and accepting everything as it is and everyone as they are."

"I Transcend judgment and shift to a higher level of mindfulness."

"I Empower myself and others to be an example of integrity and a source for positive change."

# *Karianne Munstedt*

**Karianne Munstedt Portrait**

*H*eart Word: Real / When we're real, open, honest, and vulnerable, that's when the real human connection takes place. That's what the world needs more of—people being themselves, people being real, and people being beautifully imperfect.

Karianne Munstedt is a portrait photographer in Phoenix, Arizona. She is an artist and nurturer, fiercely motivated by using her talents to make women feel confident, empowered, and whole. Growing up with an abusive role model left her filled with fear. She countered this by attempting to be perfect, but never took the time to understand who she was. She continued down a path of perfection that led her to a marriage, a job, and other endeavors that weren't right for her.

Karianne started a journey to get to know herself in her 30s. On her spiritual journey, she connected back to the thing that brought her joy as a child ... photography. She discovered an innate talent to capture a person's true inner beauty. In 2018, she left her full-time corporate job to focus on what brings her joy ... her portrait business.

# Real Is the New Perfect

## By Karianne Munstedt

As a child, I believed in perfection.

In 1965, Professor Marc Hollender defined perfectionism as: "…demanding of oneself or others a higher quality of performance than is required by the situation. Perfectionism most commonly develops in an insecure child who needs approval, acceptance, and affection from parents who are difficult to please. Later perfectionism combats self-belittlement."

More recently, Brené Brown defined perfectionism as: "…a way of thinking that says this: 'If I look perfect, live perfect, work perfect, I can avoid or minimize criticism, blame, and ridicule.' It's a shield that we carry around, hoping that it will keep us from being hurt."

Those definitions described me perfectly.

To me, most of all, being perfect meant not getting in trouble. I saw what being in trouble looked like, and I didn't want any part of that. I took that to the extreme and became perfect at EVERYTHING. I was the perfect older sister, getting perfect grades, excelling in sports, and taking on leadership roles. As a teenager, it was modeled to me that a perfect body was the preferable body type, so I started dieting. I did all of the things that I was supposed to do to receive approval and affection not only from my parents, but also from teachers and other persons of influence—mostly males.

During these formative years, I also had the notion of the perfect outside modeled for me. If you have a nice house, nice cars, nice things, and go on nice vacations, and everyone looks pretty, then everyone will think you/your family is perfect.

As a young adult, I followed that model. I applied for perfect jobs and was hired; I bought a brand-new car and designer clothes so I would look successful. Later, I bought big homes so others would be envious of my success. I painstakingly obsessed over perfectly decorating every square inch of them. Even the walls were painted with the perfect shade of color. I had a perfect wedding, too. While it may have looked perfect on the outside, it was far from perfect on the inside.

## The Other Side of Perfectionism

Perfectionism was just a way of life for me. I kept at it for so many years because I never knew any other way of doing things.

What did this amazing perfectionism get me?
Isolation/no deep relationships
Sexual assault that I thought was my fault
An eating disorder
Never knowing the real me
Unrealistic expectations of those around me
Fear of any little bit of negativity or rejection
Debt

## Isolation/no deep relationships

Perfection kept me closed off to forming true relationships. I was never ever able to be 100% myself and be vulnerable with coworkers, friends, and potential romantic relationships. I had this habit of putting on the perfect smile and asking just the right level of shallow questions so that I would still look like I cared, but never getting too deep. Once, at a photography club meeting, one of the other members asked me how I was. I replied, "Fine." I asked in a very superficial way as I flitted away to do the same with the next person, "How are you?" He started to actually answer, then said to me, "Oh, you don't really care anyway." I never talked to him again, and soon after, left that photography group. I was so ashamed and embarrassed, and mortified that others thought the same of me.

When my brother moved back to our home state, it was an incredible opportunity to develop a relationship with my new sister-in-law. Did I take advantage of that? No. I hardly took any time to get to know her at all. I was too busy decorating my big home, repainting walls, and pursuing degrees to show how smart I was.

I was afraid that if I let anybody in, they would see a crack and this huge illusion of perfection would just fall away. I knew that I wasn't actually perfect. I had no self-confidence, a wealth of self-doubt, depression, and an eating disorder. I didn't want anyone to see that. So, I kept people very far away from me. I isolated myself by staying home for the most part. I didn't attend many social gatherings because I would have actually had to have a conversation with people. I was afraid that if I didn't say the perfect thing or have the perfect quip or the perfect answer, I would look stupid.

I had the perfect façade of being a really smart person. I protected that with everything I had. Looking stupid was just about the worst thing that I could experience, so I did everything in my power to always appear to be the smartest person in the room.

## Sexual assault

Around the time of my college graduation, I was out celebrating and got completely drunk. The next thing I knew, it was the middle of the night, and I was on a golf course with two of my college classmates, and I was having sex with them. Rather, they were having sex with me. I thought it was my fault. I was a stupid girl who got way too drunk. I drank so much that I have no memory other than being at the party, then being on the golf course, and some of what was happening at the time, and what came after. I felt so much shame around this occurrence that I buried it deep and didn't realize what it actually was (rape) until nearly 20 years later.

## Eating disorder

When I was in high school, I noticed that my father seemed to be happier with my mother when she was thin, so I decided that I wanted to be thin as well. I never felt thin. I hung out with girls who were shorter and had smaller bodies than me. Even though I was very athletic and just had a different body type than them, I still felt like the big one around them. My mom tried/joined every weight loss fad/program out there, and I joined right along with her. My normal body became a lean body. I was really happy about that. I was following the program perfectly and achieving the perfect body that I thought would please others. Little did I know, I was using dieting as a way to self soothe, and it wasn't sustainable. Around the time of my sexual assault, my undereating became overeating. Sugar and carbs literally had the power to push sad emotions down deep into my belly. When emotions surrounding shame, embarrassment, and not feeling good or smart enough surfaced, I would stuff myself with sugary foods to push those emotions back down into the depths of my body. This made me feel like I was in control, although, of course, my eating was out of control. But no one got to see that. All they saw was the perfect, put-together person. I developed a Compulsive Overeating Disorder that is still a huge part of my life today.

## Never knowing the real me

I spent all my time trying to be perfect, so people wouldn't know the real me, and yet, I didn't even know who the real me was. All I knew was that being perfect meant not getting into trouble. Having opinions that differed from my father meant getting into trouble, so I therefore didn't develop any opinions on politics or religion. In fact, I spent the first 30 years of my life not having any actual opinions on anything of value at all. But I did learn to judge others. For example, I had a best friend who went on food stamps to make ends meet. I had learned that people who used food stamps were taking advantage of the system. I began to view my best friend through a judgment that was not even my own, and soon after, our relationship ended.

## Unrealistic expectations of those around me

I used to think, "If I am perfect, then I expect everyone around me to be perfect." And by perfect, I meant MY version of perfect, not their version. I formed quick judgments about others based on my own perfectionist ideals. For example, around the time I bought my car (dark blue), a friend also bought a new car. Hers was red. I saw the color red as being very showy and attention-grabbing, and I likened her choice in car color to her as a person. In my perfect world, it was better to be blue (which I likened to being chill and practical) rather than red (showy and aggressive). I judged my friend as being less than based on the color of the car she purchased.

## The fear of negativity

A coworker was frustrated with me one day and said, "We can't all be perfect like you are, Kari." I was enraged that he would say something like that to me. I was also mortified that he saw my striving for perfection as negative. Didn't he understand that I used my perfection to NOT get in trouble? Perfectionism was a way to receive approval and affection from those around me, and what he said to me was the complete opposite of that. I wanted only positive affirmations. Getting any feedback that showed me as less than perfect sent me into a spiral of self-loathing and shame.

## Debt

The perfectionist lifestyle not only required me to have nice new cars, clothes, shoes, and immaculately decorated big homes, I needed the education to go along with it. In my quest for achievement, I decided to go back to school for a master's degree, then a doctorate degree, then another master's degree, and then another master's degree (I only finished one). I didn't feel smart at all, and to compensate, I kept going back to school as I was desperate to show everyone else how smart I was. I also didn't know myself at all, so each time I went back to school, it ended up not feeling right, so I quit. All of this looked good on the outside, but it was all financed through credit cards and loans. I ended up with a huge pile of debt, a short-sale on a house, creditors calling every day, and SO MUCH SHAME.

## The Spark That Started the Change

As I entered my late twenties, things started feeling not right to me. I felt like I couldn't hold it together any longer. And I started to see something that scared me more than anything:

I didn't like this perfect version of me.

So, I decided to see a counselor. I don't know how I even came to that realization, as asking for help was not something that had ever been modeled for me. It turns out, that was the best thing that I could have ever done for myself.

Somehow that initial gut feeling of needing help turned into a six-year counseling relationship. In that time, we broke down so many of my barriers. I learned how to be real and how to be vulnerable. I started noticing that I didn't have to be perfect and that there were things in my life that were not healthy for me emotionally.

During those six years of counseling, I started taking my life into my own hands. I started figuring out what I wanted in life. I recognized there were some areas in my life I wasn't happy with. It was HUGE to finally realize that I had the power to actually make changes in my life. I let go of unhealthy friendships. I let go of a very destructive family relationship. I even let go of the unhealthy marriage that I was in.

My perfectionist tendencies still showed up throughout my counseling. I wanted to help others in the way my counselor helped me. So, the perfect student in me decided I wanted to become a counselor. True to form, once I said I was going to do something, the perfectionist in me always did it. So, I applied to social work programs, and I got accepted to one of the top schools (of course I did!). But the thing is, it never felt quite right. I still didn't really know who I was and what I truly wanted in life. I just jumped at the chance to try something different and meet a new group of people to prove how perfect I was.

At about the same time that I got accepted into social work school, I met David. Our relationship took off very quickly, and within six months, we were married. He and his daughter were local, so I put my social work plans on hold to finally start the family that I had always wanted. (David and I have now been married for seven years and have a son together.)

As I continued in counseling, I finally started to get a sense of my true self and started to examine areas of my life where I wasn't feeling right. The more I thought about it, the more I realized that a career as a counselor wasn't the way for me to go.

One thing I did know was that I wanted to help people. Along this counseling journey that I was on, I started to connect back to the things that brought me joy as a child. For me, this was photography. I was always the child with a camera in my hand, so I picked it up again. I discovered not only a rekindled love, but an innate talent to capture a person's true inner beauty.

## *The Flame That Burned the Whole Perfection House of Cards Down*

I had my own boudoir photo shoot, and during that session, the Universe delivered the message that I needed to hear. The woman who was doing my hair and makeup told me about a photographer named Sue Bryce. Sue was apparently an amazing portrait photographer and specialized in photographing women so they could really see their own beauty. When I got home, I looked up Sue Bryce, and her images were stunning. I fell in love with the way she was helping women feel empowered and beautiful in their own skin. I signed up for one of her workshops, and then I had the opportunity to also be photographed by her.

Going into the session, I was filled with so much anxiety. My clothes weren't perfect enough; my body wasn't perfect enough. The negative voices in my head were in full blast and saying, "Kari, you're too fat to be photographed. Kari, no one wants to photograph you. Kari, who do you think you are?"

But still, I knew I needed to do this. So, I took a deep breath, tuned out the negative voices the best that I could, and went for it. And guess what happened?

I had fun. The photographer made me feel at ease and really did want to photograph me. I left the session holding my head a little higher. And when I saw the final portraits of myself, I saw the real me—not the outer me—the me in my soul looking back at me. That moment changed everything for me. I knew right then I wanted EVERY WOMAN to have this same experience and to feel this kind of confidence.

I was able to see the REAL me in my portraits because I dropped the notion of perfection and went into that session as MYSELF. I saw how much better I looked and felt when I dropped the pretense and showed up as my imperfect self.

## *Real Is the New Perfect*

Perfect is a word that we should take out of the dictionary.

The word perfect is an illusion. I'm sure that it had a place in its origins, but we started applying the word to standards of beauty and life. It makes us always want to strive for and achieve more, and not in a positive way. Striving for perfection tells us that we aren't good enough at something now.

It's grasping for the next level, thinking things will get better if only we can get there. As we strive to have the perfect body, perfection is telling us that our body isn't good or worthy enough as it is right now. As we strive to have the perfect, successful business, we're telling ourselves that our business isn't good enough just as it is right now. As we strive to have the perfect marriage, perfection is telling us that our marriage isn't good enough as it is right now. We think that by achieving perfection, our troubles will disappear. That is an illusion. Striving for perfection creates the problems in the first place.

Striving for perfection leads us to comparing ourselves to others in an unhealthy manner. We see everyone's perfect on social media. We think we must be failures if our reality doesn't match their perfectly curated posts. We know that "comparison is the thief of joy" and can lead us down the rabbit hole. Comparison and striving for perfection is part of what led me to an eating disorder. For others, it leads to depression, drinking, drugs, other addictions, and even suicide.

I get it. Being real can seem hard and scary. We might have to let people in and see things about us that we might not even like about ourselves. We have to get more in tune with those things and just realize that it's okay to be photographed when you have lumps and bumps on your body. It's okay to have problems in your marriage. It's okay to be struggling in your business. We don't have to hide it because when we're real, open, honest, and vulnerable, that's when the real human connection takes place.

When we do this, that's when we realize it's okay. That's when we see that people accept us for ourselves. We step out of that isolating shell that we've been living in. We step away from those addictions that have been holding us back from being our true selves. And that's what the world needs more of: people being themselves, people being real, and people being beautifully imperfect.

When you are vulnerable, the truth is people might turn away from you. If they do, it will hurt. However, you will see they weren't really your people in the first place. If someone is going to not like you for being you, then they're not your people.

As Glennon Doyle says, "We can do hard things." We can turn to a friend and ask for help. We can put a picture of ourselves out on social media that shows our lumps and bumps. We can turn to a coach to help us with our businesses. By casting the perfectionism aside and being honest and real with others, our lives will change for the better.

Perfectionism, thank you for serving me. You kept me safe. I am now ready to release you. I am ready to move into the next phase of my life with honesty and vulnerability. I am ready to move on to being REAL.

Real is the new Perfect.

# Kate Weeks

**Business Development Manager at Resurrection University**

*H*eart Word: Strength / The reason I chose strength is throughout my life I have had to find the strength to move forward.

Kate Weeks is a business development manager at Resurrection University where she develops partnerships with clinical partners and manages clinical placements. She graduated from the University of Wisconsin Oshkosh with a bachelor's degree in Elementary Education and a minor in Language Arts in 2006. She then continued on with her education and graduated with her

Master of Business Administration and Education Management from Keller Graduate School of Management. After graduation, she moved to Chicago and lived there for nine years. In her copious free time, she enjoys spending time with her daughter and family, dancing, reading, and writing.

# Strength and Resurrection

## By Kate Weeks

I have always wanted to be a good wife, mother, sister, daughter, and friend. When you wear so many different hats, the lines at times get blurred. I think of my life and how many obstacles I have overcome and how they have now shaped me to be the woman that I am today.

I came into this world via the Neonatal Intensive Care Unit (NICU), diagnosed with Congenital Cytomegalovirus (CMV) and jaundice. I contracted CMV during gestation. Once you are infected, your body retains the virus for life. The odds were not in my favor. Some babies have health problems at birth while others develop them later. Signs and symptoms include congenital abnormalities, being susceptible to low birth weight, microcephaly, seizures, rubella, jaundice, hearing loss, vision impairment, and learning disabilities.

I was baptized in the hospital where my mother worked as a pediatric nurse at Cardinal Glennon Children's Hospital in St Louis, Missouri. In the 1980's, it was unknown if babies would survive being sick with CMV. My mom had contracted the virus while working on the pediatric unit. My parents knew the outcomes of what my life could be like being born with CMV.

Throughout my childhood, adolescence, and into high school, I struggled with school. I had supportive parents who did everything they possibly could to help me be successful in life. It wasn't until I was in my last year of my elementary education studies in college that I started to see similarities between my students and me. They were struggling with understanding speech in noisy environments, following directions, and distinguishing between sounds. I realized I too had struggled with these issues my whole life. I then tested to see if I had the same outcomes as my students. When the results came back, I was sitting in the Dean of Education's office and she was reviewing the results with me. She said, "Kate, you have an Auditory Processing Disability (APD)." At that very moment, my entire struggle and anguish over the years came full circle. I always envied those that could remember everything so easily, and I thought I must be dumb.

Through self-discovery, I reevaluated what my path/journey would be in education. My life then took a hard left. President George W. Bush, Jr. had just implemented the No Child Left Behind Act. At the time, the Administration started to mandate that all teachers nationwide be measured on their competencies via a comprehensive exam prior to receiving their teaching certificate and graduating. The University of Wisconsin, Oshkosh was offering a test-out option for all current students to take the Praxis Exam. We would be considered the "testing" models. This meant that the 2006 graduating class would be given the "pass" option for the exam, and granted their teaching certificates. I was up all night studying for the exam.

The next day, I went to take the Praxis Exam and realized I had mixed up the times. They would not let me take the test. The door was shut on my career at that moment as I would not be able to graduate with a full certified license to teach. I pleaded with the Dean of Education; I wrote letters to the Board of Education and the Provost to no avail. My dreams of becoming a teacher and six years of unbelievable hard work were literally thrown out the window because of one exam. Today, this exam "requirement" for teachers is now being challenged and thrown out in many states.

I had a bachelor's degree and didn't know what to do with it. The recession hit. I was without a job, and the student loans were coming due. My roommate and I were in the process of looking for jobs in Chicago, and I landed a position at a university doing admissions work. Through this job, I met my lifelong friends and started my career path. I worked in many positions through admissions, academics, operations management, and now clinical coordination management. Throughout all these transitions with work, my personal life was also changing rapidly.

The first milestone was a joyous and beautiful wedding day. I was filled with joy and peace as I walked down the aisle to the man that I loved for six years. Not only was I becoming his bride, I was now his wife. To have all of our loved ones around us on that special day was the greatest testament to how we brought two families together. Six months after our wedding, we went on a honeymoon to celebrate our nuptials.

Baby fever was in the air, and we began to try to conceive in October 2016. I was discouraged after three months of trying. I wondered whether we would ever have a baby. Let's be honest, I was not getting any younger at this point. On my 34th birthday, I woke up early and took a pregnancy test. I held my breath, hoping and praying that this would be it. The test was a faint two lines of pink. I couldn't believe it and woke up my husband. I said, "We are going to be parents!" The look on his face was utter shock. He said he was so happy and excited. He then went back to bed. At the time, I didn't think anything of it, because I was so unbelievably happy that I was pregnant. Then the little one gave us a scare on New Year's Eve. I started to spot, and I thought I was having a miscarriage. We went in for an emergency ultrasound, and that is when we first saw our little nugget. She was just a little round ball of joy on the screen. That is when I knew my primary purpose in life was to be this little one's mother.

After that minor scare, my pregnancy was great. We were both working and going about our lives and excited to be parents. On the day of my second baby shower, it was 90 degrees and hotter than all get out. I was feeling very pregnant and just out of sorts. I had been to the doctor earlier that week. (My husband was on a business trip in Philadelphia.) It was not my original doctor as she was on vacation. I had been suffering from Braxton Hicks, which is the tightening of the abdomen causing false contractions. They are extremely uncomfortable and feel like menstrual cramps. I was nauseous and vomiting. The doctor thought maybe I ate something bad and told me to go home and rest. At the baby shower, I could barely read the congratulatory cards and was feeling very lightheaded. I just thought it was the weather.

My little sister was staying to take our maternity pictures that afternoon. She took photos all around the park, and I was just so happy to be capturing these moments with my husband and baby girl. After the photo session, we came home and ate some delicious pizza. I remember lying down and thinking, "I am just exhausted." Our 14-year-old German Shepherd, Thunder, would not leave my side and then came right up to my stomach. He kept nudging me to get up, so I thought he needed to go out. I then stood up and went to the door to let him out. He just stood there looking at me like, "I don't need to go, mom." So, I shut the door, and then I went to the bathroom for it felt like someone was doing a tap dance on my bladder. On the way to the bathroom, I peed in my underwear. As I was seven months pregnant, I frequently had extra underwear on hand. Then I looked at Thunder's head on my leg and his puppy eyes. I thought to myself, "What is going on with him tonight?" Then, I knew. It was ME!

We went to bed that night at 9:00 pm, just exhausted from the day. Just like every other pregnant woman at seven months, I could not get comfortable. I was up moving around getting some water and the Braxton Hicks began. I then thought about how intense those pains were.

So, what does every woman do who is paranoid and anxiety driven? She opens her laptop to WebMD. I then proceeded to call my mother and started timing my Braxton Hicks now believed to be contractions. To my surprise, they were now five minutes apart, and panic started to set in. I screamed for my husband to wake up and call the doctor.

At this point, I had taken a shower to supposedly calm my Braxton Hicks. I got dressed and I was in the process of packing my bag when I felt this unbelievable pressure to go to the bathroom. I sat on the toilet thinking I had to go number two. The nurse on the phone that was paging the doctor told my husband to get me off the toilet. Well, too late, blood was everywhere, and I was in full-on labor. I couldn't move, my body was frozen just sitting there on the toilet. It took every ounce of my strength to get me on the bathroom floor. The pain was so immense. My dog, Thunder, was all up in my business and then suddenly, the gush of water came like a lightning force and my baby was on her way. I kept saying I don't want to have her in this bathroom on the floor. My husband was now on the phone with 911, and the ambulance was en route. I was trying to remember to breathe and focus on something like I learned in my birthing class. I kept staring at the cross-stitch picture in my bathroom and thinking, "Grandma I hope you are here." I could feel my daughter turning and thought, "Oh dear Lord, she is coming and fast."

There was a total of seven emergency medical technicians (EMTs) that helped carry me down the stairs. I kept saying, "I cannot get blood on this new carpet!" My clothes were being torn off me while I was on the stretcher. Unopened baby shower gifts were on the floor. We weren't ready for her yet! The doors opened wide to this sterile vehicle that was now going to transport me and my sweet girl to the hospital five minutes away. The EMT, Diaz, was trying to find my veins to start an IV. I kept telling him,

"No, you can't find it in my arms, you need to do it in my hand!" The EMT who was driving kept asking about my contractions and whether we were timing them. I said, "They are five minutes apart." I wondered why they weren't keeping track of this information after looking at the digital clock and breathing. Why was I doing all of this while lying on a stretcher keeping my baby inside me? One EMT said, "Ma'am, you need to keep the baby in as long as possible." I looked at him and said, "I don't want to have her in this ambulance, but she is just about in between my legs. Tell your driver to step on it and to quit going over so many bumps!"

Staring at the clock yelling obscenities, we finally made it to the ER at Edward Hospital. I was then greeted with more nurses and doctors. The ER doctor checked me, and I about decked him in the face for how awful that felt! The hallways seemed endless to the OB floor, with a sea of people in one room. I was being lifted on the bed, my legs were placed in stirrups, there was equipment everywhere, and so many faces of people I didn't know. I felt so unbelievably alone at that moment thinking how I was going to do this. I asked repeatedly, "Can I have some drugs, please?" The nurse would respond, "No, sweetie, you are 100% effaced." I was like oh sweet Lord, this pain is just so overwhelming, I am going to pass out. I don't do well with pain, but to deliver a baby without meds was not a part of my birthing plan. I kept searching for something or someone to focus on, then my husband appeared. I shouted, "Where have you been? I can't do this!" I was in full on panic mode and I needed to push.

This baby was coming, and they wanted me to wait. I said, "I can't wait anymore. She is coming fast and is going to fall out if we don't do something." So, they brought in the OB ER doctor. I looked at my husband with complete fear in my eyes. He grabbed my hand and said, "You need to push." I pushed once and the pain shot through my body as if I was being stabbed a thousand times repeatedly. I pushed again, and then utter relief. My daughter was out and people were scrambling everywhere.

I couldn't hear her! I kept asking, "How is she?" I couldn't get an answer from anyone. At that moment, it felt like the world had stopped. I was in slow motion watching the doctors and nurses work to save our little girl's life. Then in a flash, she was wrapped up in a white blanket with little feet on them. I held her for 30 seconds; the nurses took two photos of the three of us, and then she was whisked off to the NICU. I told my husband, "Go with her and keep her safe!" Then, just like that, I was alone again with a room full of strangers. As I lie there getting stitched up and wondering what had happened to make her come so early, I was then inundated with questions and forms to sign. It was for my daughter's care which involved testing her oxygen levels, giving her steroids, and possible life support. I took a deep breath and said, "Do whatever it takes to keep her alive." The flood gates opened, and the tears just flowed and didn't stop.

The whirlwind of our daughter's birth would change the course of our lives. We spent 15 hours a day for three straight weeks in the NICU where our beautiful daughter, Savannah "Savvy" June Weeks, fought every single minute to live. She was only 32 weeks old and was four pounds and 11 ounces. This was the biggest challenge my husband and I had faced in our lives. We remained positive and our sweet angel came home at 35 weeks old. It was the best birthday present my husband ever received. We were so excited to have her home!

She grew stronger every day. Breastfeeding took its toll on me. I was having a hard time adjusting with the low supply of milk and mommy guilt. We continued as we went through the motions of work, family events, a baptism, doctor's appointments, and trying to figure out how to pay all of the medical bills. I began to notice the stress was taking its toll on my husband. I was now back to work full-time. Due to me leaving abruptly before my maternity leave was to officially start, things were in disarray at work, too. I was also struggling with major anxiety and managing the stress of it all.

My husband's career was taking off, and he started to travel more internationally. We knew this could be a great opportunity, and I supported him on this new journey. He was traveling at least three weeks each month and taking on new projects. I was raising our daughter, coordinating care, managing the household, and working full-time. I was extremely exhausted and was staying with my parents while he was away so I could have additional support. During this time, I started to notice a slight change with my husband. He was more aggressive, arrogant, and had very little patience with me or Savvy.

My job was being phased out and there was a job opening for an event planner position. I wanted the job because it could open doors for me to eventually start my own event planning business. The only downfall was that it was an hour and a half away from our home. We had planned on moving in the next couple of years so my husband said I should apply for the position and we would figure everything out.

I got the job. I had only been in the role for a week when on Friday, October 2nd I saw on the 6:00 am news there was a mass shooting on the Las Vegas Strip at the Route 91 Harvest Music Festival. My husband was just a block from where the shooting took place. My stomach dropped, and I picked up the phone and called my husband repeatedly. When he didn't answer, I thought, "Oh my God, I lost him!" He eventually picked up and told me that he was nowhere near the incident, and was in his hotel room. He was extremely vague with me and I thought something was off. He was coming home the next day.

For the next six months, my husband was distant with me and barely interacted with Savvy. He was angry, resentful, reckless, drinking, smoking, and gambling more. It was then that I started to put the pieces together. There were messages on his phone from a random number, emails, and pictures of his company vice president (VP) on his phone. I wondered why she was in all these photos and was reaching out to him at all hours of the day and night. I confronted him five separate times about having an affair. He made up all kinds of stories and lies. I, of course, believed him because he was my husband. He made me feel like I was going crazy.

We then started to work on our marriage, and planned our special day out for our 4th wedding anniversary. We had a great day celebrating at the horse races, dinner, and then went home to play with our sweet little girl. It was then that I told him I was quitting my job and focusing on our marriage and family. That week I put my two weeks' notice in and found another position in Chicago.

It was the Friday of Mother's Day weekend and I was on my way back to Chicago to spend the weekend with my in-laws and my husband. I had called him, and he said he would be on the train at 5:00 pm and would meet us at his parent's house. Then two hours later, he sent a text message saying he wouldn't be on the 5:00 pm train and would be taking an Uber home instead. It was then that I knew he was with her. Savvy was in bed asleep and I told my in-laws that I had to do some last-minute shopping.

I was on the phone with my sister-in-law as I drove over to our condo. In the guest parking area, there was his VP's minivan sitting in stall B-69. With my heart racing, I now knew that my gut was right. I sat there and waited for three hours. Meanwhile, at 8:00 pm my husband called me to say he was on his way home. I said, "I can't wait to see you honey, I love you. The Uber black SUV pulled up to her car. I was expecting both of them to get out of the SUV, but she was the only one that was dropped off. I then realized my husband was being dropped off at my in-law's house.

He would soon figure out where I was. She was dressed in her Chicago Cubs attire and looked drunk. I stepped out of my car and I prayed for strength as I approached the woman who was sleeping with my husband.

I confronted her outside in the blistering cold as tears streamed down my face. She confirmed my fears from the past year. The affair started when our daughter was eight months old and she loved him. She told me that she was leaving her husband and was filing for divorce. She has four daughters of her own and I thought to myself, those poor girls. She then made it about herself and shared how she was in an abusive relationship. I then looked at her and said, "You always have an out and you should protect those girls. No matter what, get your stuff and move out. You always have a choice to leave, but my husband is not that choice." She claimed she never meant to hurt me or my daughter. I said, "Well, you should have thought of that before you befriended me, invited us to your home for family events, slept in my bed, and betrayed my trust." She then went on to say how wonderful my husband was and how great he was at work. I said, "I know all of this, and he is my husband."

In a blur, I then proceeded to leave our home and drove back to my in-laws. I remember walking into the house out of breath and asking my father-in-law, "Where is he?" He said, "I told him you were out. He said that you would know where to find him." I said, "Oh yes, I will find him." I called him in a fit of rage and he said he was on his way back to his parent's house. When he returned, I confronted him about the entire situation, and he was angry with me for confronting her outside of our home. It was there that he proceeded to tell me he wanted to go on this new path/journey with her. I was in complete and utter shock that this man I had loved for ten years was saying he no longer wanted to be with me while we were at his parent's home.

I could hear Savvy crying upstairs and my mother-in-law was consoling her while she sobbed. I asked my husband, "So, you want a divorce?" He couldn't even say it. He then walked out of the living room, down the hall, and out the door. My world came crashing down. The cry that I let out was like nothing I had ever heard before in my life. I didn't sleep, eat, or move for two days. I couldn't even hold or look at my daughter. I didn't want to get out of bed. My entire body had just shut down and I was a mess.

The only light that kept me going was my daughter and the new little life that was growing inside me. My world had shifted and tilted upside down in so many ways. Then, life started to balance out with work, meeting new friends, and trying to figure out this new normal. Throughout all this turmoil and stress, I miscarried our baby. I hadn't told anyone at this point, not even my husband, and I was going to keep it that way.

It is time to focus on what I need, and how to be a better mother, daughter, sister, and friend. I am taking my life, my daughter, and never looking back.

Life gives us some bad lemons at times, but when we get the good lemons, we have to hold onto those. When we make that lemonade and share it with our loved ones, that is what makes it worth the wait. Strength and resurrection make some wicked good lemonade.

# Holly Pasut

**Inspirational, Motivational Speaker,
Keynote Speaker, Author Blogger**

*H*eart Word: Flawmazing: This might sound harsh, but not everyone is going to like you. This fantasy is delusional because it's simply impossible. No matter how hard I've tried to become the best version of myself, I will always be flawed. However, my life experiences both good and bad motivated me to forge meaning. Character is always being revealed and how one finds pure gold after the stumble and fall is amazing. The world will be a better place for everyone when you find the perfect tension in holding your flaws while knowing you're still amazing.

Holly Pasut was a nationally recognized real estate agent in the booming southeast market. Perseverance, knowledge, relationship building, and trust led her to be among the top agents in the county. Then she spent one year in federal prison for the involvement in a mortgage fraud case that was one of the largest investigations in the United States.

When you think of prison, you think criminal. Holly takes full responsibility for her decisions, but had she known the risks and understood the widespread scheme going on behind the scenes, her life would be much different today.

Today, Holly speaks about her path from an icon agent to a federal prison cell with white-collar professionals and university students around the country. Her audiences are awakened by the risks professionals take, often without even knowing it. Topics include big lessons from federal prison, critical thinking errors, recognizing your inner voice, and changing your mindset.

A life group leader, certified life coach, and volunteer for several ministries and second chance organizations, Holly encourages socially stigmatized groups to live beyond their stigma. She is the founder of "Picnic Table Talks" which encourages authentic conversations, humility, and faith. Holly is a loving mother to three adult children who inspire her on a daily basis. Quiet morning meditations are part of her spiritual regime, along with regular workouts, long walks, and a few sets of tennis. She does confess, however, she is easily distracted by music.

# From Hell and Back

## By Holly Pasut

It is both strange and humbling that among millions of authors, I was asked to be a part of this book. More than likely, you too have a story that would resonate with others. Frankly, I get tired of my past sufferings, challenges, and difficulties, but by sharing our burdens, we create fellowship for others in their darkest times.

Making lemonade requires a bitter mixture of undesirable ingredients. They may be unimaginable, eventful, unexpected, and unfair, but these lemons are known as life, which surrounds all of us. We are bonded together experiencing a mixture of the same tragedies. Mine may differ from yours, but it's the wisdom we gain that will change the way we see the world forever.

The focus of my contribution is not to rehash stories of sadness from past trials. For me, it's creating an awareness of the freedom we have to choose to see the world through a different colored lens because of our pain and loss.

## It Starts Here

My first husband and I faced infertility. We participated in every medical test and procedure known to medicine at that time. I was fixated and obsessed with this problem and found it unbearable to look at glowing mothers and their beautiful babies. I used to enjoy walking through the baby department, imagining adorning our baby in the precious clothing so nicely displayed. However, over time, the continued negative test results added to my hopelessness and pessimistic thinking. I became the poster child for dispiritedness and irrational thinking, consequently leading to a marriage of detachment. In hindsight, I divorced a good man.

My second husband, Alessandro (Sandro) Pasut, was born and raised in Venice, Italy; he was charismatic and strikingly handsome. His star quality had a magical way of lighting up a room upon entering; people seemingly gravitated towards him. His Italian accent was thick, and he made a great effort to find the correct English words to describe his feelings. Once, he told me he loved me very much, and after every day that went by, he wanted to add another "very."

I felt obligated to explain to Sandro the difficulty I had experienced regarding conceiving a child. Surprisingly, he didn't seem upset or concerned, but in turn, expressed his desire to travel the world. The life of a jet setter was never on my bucket list, but why not?

When we returned from a picture-perfect honeymoon in Italy, I found myself out of sorts … and yep, we had conceived! Sooner than expected, we had three children within five years. God can do what doctors can't!

## The First Ingredient Rears Its Ugly Head

Apparently, I wasn't the only person getting knocked up! Infidelity found its way into our marriage. When I confided in my father for support, I was (pardon me) hoping he would shoot Sandro. In contrast, my mother told me pencils had erasers because everyone makes mistakes, and since I had two children at the time, I needed to find forgiveness. Not exactly what I wanted to hear, but I knew she was right. While extending grace, we conceived and had baby number three.

Our marriage became strained and laborious. I became suspicious of his behavior. His busy travel schedule was a breeding ground for extramarital affairs. Due to his travel schedule and a combination of other things, inevitably, we became more and more distant. Nine months later, Sandro committed suicide.

Widowed with three children, devastated, lost, and wanting to kill him myself, I had to find a way to survive. For most of my children's lives, I refrained from explaining the whole truth about their father's death. I told them it was an accident, not suicide. My decision was to protect them from feelings of abandonment. I also didn't want them to feel suicide was ever an option in their own lives. Once they became adults, their questions became detailed and deliberate. This weighed on me, knowing the day would come when I would owe them the true story.

They each responded in varying ways. Rocky sought solace as he processed this new information, but was not entirely surprised by what I said. He always had a feeling there was more to the story. Alexi became suspicious and guarded as if I had more secrets, and Zico was mournful that I had to endure the tragedy. It was heartbreaking in a heartwarming way to witness my kids display such showing compassion towards one another after knowing the whole story behind their father's suicide. Over time, they showed a reasonable understanding of my decision to wait until they had become adults to explain.

I didn't know how to be a dad; I didn't teach the boys "dad stuff" like starting a lawnmower, using power tools, or changing a flat tire. However, they learned other things, such as speaking from the heart, seeking to understand, coming from curiosity, humility-like communication, articulating, sensitivity, and how to do their own laundry! My daughter, Alexi, will never have the memory of sitting on her father's lap or reminiscing about an evening at a father-daughter dance. Having said that, it's important to her that her own children experience everything she was denied.

The possibility of being widowed never occurred to me. Widowed was for old ladies! Life gave me my first gulp of unfairness and a jolt of reality. It was especially agonizing to acknowledge that my innocent young children would grow up without knowing their father.

There were countless days I wanted to trade strength and perseverance in for someone to take care of me. I don't think people meant harm, but in attempting to be compassionate, they would refer to my children as burdens. Any truthful mother will confess that kids can drive you crazy, but despite the chaos and commotion, I never considered them to be burdens, but always and forever my gifts from God. Today, my children tell me I am the strongest and most courageous person they know.

## One Year Later

My mother was unique, high-spirited, and loved to dance anywhere and everywhere! Her thick blonde hair was always styled and bouncing. Her unusual green eyes were trance-inducing. But her greatest gift was her thirst for life … intoxicating and noticed by all.

In her early 60's, she was diagnosed with what doctors referred to as Epstein-Barr Disease or Chronic Fatigue Syndrome. She eagerly underwent every medical and non-medical test known to man. Actively seeking to be part of her own rescue and healing, she welcomed the MRIs, blood tests, blood drains, body poking, strange new foods, vitamins and minerals, and hypnosis. With grave disappointment, there was no known cure or relief for her discomfort.

Time quietly robbed her. There were days you could see depression and worry deep inher soul, while other days were full of passion and inspiration. It was as if watching her battle like a prize-winning champion. Ultimately, her bed became her life and prison cell. Tick tock, the days passed by as she continuously watched the ceiling fan go round and round. Her body was failing her, yet her mind was sharp. I remember the day she told me she felt like a prisoner in her own body, and she could not escape. Without the ability to fill her pockets up with sunshine, she lost her zest for life. My glamorous and spunky mother made a final decision.

A year after my husband committed suicide, my mother elected to do the same. She quietly swallowed pills she had been storing up for a long time and finally freed herself from the life of hell she was imprisoned to endure. I would never condone suicide, yet in my mother's case, I understood. I like to think she is dancing in heaven today.

Some days I try to remember my mother's voice. I long to hear her at times, and I wonder if I would recognize her voice. I do remember all my mother's quirky expressions. I recall the fun and frustration, teaching her how to disco dance while cleaning up the kitchen after dinner, and listening to her sing and tell jokes. What I do remember the most though, was her birthday—the one we celebrated after she was gone.

It was March, and one of my kids reminded me it was Nona's birthday. I gently responded that Nona was dead and unable to have a birthday party. Well, I couldn't have been more wrong. "Mom, just because Nona is not here doesn't mean we can't celebrate her birthday!" With birthday cake, ice cream, candles, and music, we joyfully honored her birthday and danced liked popping popcorn. My mom would have certainly approved.

A cause for celebration is not dependent on a specific time or holiday; it's an attitude and a choice. Rarely does a day go by without me being reminded of my mother, because she is in me. With the same kind of playfulness, I repeat my mother's jokes to my own friends. When I laugh, I hear her, loud and from the belly. It cannot be denied, I am easily distracted by music, and I miss my cherished dance partner, my mom.

We have consciously chosen to keep those we love alive all the more since they are not with us in the flesh. My kids carry their father with them, and I, my mother. Isn't it odd, my children, as well as myself, have lost a parent to suicide?

## The Crumble

Real estate was a career that afforded me the ability to schedule my own hours, and make enough money to provide for my family. I would be lying if I didn't admit it was also stressful and fatiguing. Often, I was negotiating offers rather than eating dinner with my family. My kids wanted to scream every time the phone rang; well, they did scream!

I was successful and financially secure. My best days were spent at the kid's hot and humid baseball games eating peanuts and cheering for our team. My adrenaline was on steroids when I watched Zico's ball soar beyond the fence for his first grand slam. A face of pure delight is ingrained in my memory today. Our house was filled with an excitement of college football, dancing, and cheerleading competitions. I had become the mother-father and loved it. The type of relationship I have with my kids today is largely due to the fact we were without a dad. I doubled up on love, discipline, and the freedom to be who God created. And then our safety net was yanked out from under our feet, and the sweetness of life began to crumble.

## *Prison*

On July 31st, 2014, I was ordered to self-surrender to Federal Prison Camp in Alderson, West Virginia. During my 14-year career as a realtor, I made many good choices and a very bad one. I trusted a group of extremely deceitful people, and as a result, I was charged with conspiracy to commit mortgage fraud and money laundering. I was sentenced to 21 months. I was no longer Holly, the trusted real estate broker; now I was inmate number 27879058.

I had a choice to either plead guilty or go to trial. Both choices were horrifying, but I had to pick one. The reality was I would serve less time if I pled guilty, so I chose the guilty plea. Shortly afterward, I went to discuss my plea with my pastor, but instead, I broke down. Gasping for air, I tried to tell the pastor I felt my faith had been tested, and I failed the test. I had honestly lost faith in humanity and unforgivably, God. The remorse and anguish I felt about my decision had begun eating me from the inside out, knowing I did not have the courage to find what would happen if I lost. For someone who loved life, and would not have ever considered suicide, I shamefully did not want to live anymore.

The pastor listened to my rambling thoughts while watching me nervously tremble. At that point, he asked me a peculiar question. He asked me to describe what a house looks like after it burned down.

I closed my eyes and timidly responded, "Well, the roof is caved in, there's shattered glass and splintered wood, remnants of the home are scattered, it's ash and sooty, it's blackish and grey ... it's demolished, unrecognizable, and it's flattened."

Then he said, "Holly, I'm going to ask you a very critical question, what's left?"

I quickly opened my eyes as I knew the answer—the foundation! He reminded me that anyone who had been through what I had gone through would probably look and feel the way I did. To his point, he then noted there was one thing nobody could have access to or take away from me—my foundation.

That scene played over and over in my mind while lying on my cozy, lumpy, metal bed in cube 44. One morning it hit me. I heard, "Get up and make something of this time in your life. Forge meaning, Holly!"

Have you ever wondered what other people pray for? I have. I'll tell you what I prayed for. I prayed for answers. I asked God not to release me until I understood why I had said yes to something I didn't want to do. I wanted to understand.

God didn't speak audibly. He didn't strike me over the head. He didn't instant message me. Instead, God answered my prayers in an unexpected way—he changed my focus. If you're praying for money, he may not give you the winning scratch-off ticket, but he will give you something to think about.

I realize I have a choice in how I live my life. I can choose to be depressed, stressed, worried, mad, or full of rage. But I might as well be dead, because at least I wouldn't feel so dreadful. I didn't want to die, I wanted to inhale life into my body and live again.

If you want joy and fulfillment out of your life, if you want change or healing, something or someone must initiate that change. Prison became my wilderness, but the pain and the suffering got my attention.

## What Makes Life Worth Living?

It's my guess you are reading this book because you have gone through something eventful or uncontrollable in your life. My father says I have a way of finding something good in the worst of circumstances. I believe we all can.

The need or drive to seek pleasure is alive and well in our society today.

Sigmund Freud, an Austrian neurologist best known for developing the theories and techniques of psychoanalysis referred to this drive as the "Pleasure Principle," also known as the "will for pleasure." But what happens when you are seeking a pleasurable family beach vacation only to find it raining, dissatisfying, and fatiguing? We are lured by the idea of seeking pleasure, yet pleasure in and of itself is always fleeting. Unfounded pleasure is disheartening.

Alfred Adler, an Austrian medical doctor and psychotherapist, weighed in on the need for power, or "striving for superiority." Obviously, this relentless pursuit is displayed in our culture today. Money, authority, status, and fame—we want it all and will do anything to get it. It's the ultimate goal. This "will for power" is unending, and if you do make it to the next level, you want more. It's never enough.

According to Viktor Frankl, an Austrian neurologist and psychiatrist as well as a Holocaust Survivor, he depicted these wills as manifestations of something missing. Have you ever felt a void in your life as if you are frolicking in the ocean, going nowhere? Have you ever felt a void in your life as if you are frolicking in the ocean, going nowhere?

Prison is not designed to be pleasurable, and the system encourages prisoners to remain inferior, far from powerful. The ladies used to say they would begin living their lives once they returned home. It may have sounded harsh, but I reminded them that prison was their home, and that their lives were still worth living. Prison allowed me the time to search my soul, my values, and realign my thought patterns. The expectation for pleasure or power did not occur to me; I accepted prison to be what it was, an earthly hell. And that hell is where I began my exploration of my inner self. Frankl believed the greatest task for any person is to find meaning in his or her life. The will to meaning comes from within. It finds you! We all experience different types of pain, some more tragic than others. The desire to find meaning will sustain us no matter how little or how much pleasure and power we experience. Meaning also helps us to endure any pain and suffering that we cannot avoid.

While in prison, I thought back to the words my mother spoke the day she said she felt like a prisoner in her own body, when her mind was free, yet her body was failing. I thought about the vast number of people who were living and thriving in society, yet were prisoners in their own minds. I wanted something different. What if I could be physically and mentally free at the same time? Nobody will give you the keys to unlock your personal prison of shame, fear, and dismay, whatever it may be. The only one who can do it is the one living inside you. You have the keys.

When the ladies said they would begin their lives once they returned home, I thought the polar opposite. If we don't take time to examine our own presence, we backslide and remain in our black hole. I decided to live a new way of thinking! I choose to be better instead of bitter. I will never permit making meaning an unachievable rainbow. I am responsible for my thoughts; nobody can take those away. Prison was my practice ground.

I also want to point out that courage is something that shields us after the fear, but not always. While my courage collapsed, pleading guilty ruined me publicly, just ask Google. But Google doesn't get to say it was fatal, because it was not fatal. The embarrassment and humility I experienced was a gift of disharmony. Necessary suffering finds the heart in everything. If you are never exposed to a dash of asymmetry, fragility, dizziness, off-centeredness, or a little off-ness, you will miss the gift of disharmony.

Even though I looked for meaning on a daily basis, not every day seemed meaningful. The best part of a bad day was knowing that tomorrow was a new one.

My kids were diligent about visiting almost every weekend. I suspected they feared I would be depressed if nobody came to see me. The summer heat, lack of sleep, and overall uneasiness took a toll on me. During a visit, I expressed my lowliness to my family. I perceived my life as living in a hole, and I believed I had hit rock bottom.

They patiently listened until my son, Rocky, responded, "Mom, we are trying to pull you out of your hole, but you gotta put your hands up and reach for us. Holes are not to be lived in, but to be climbed out of." In retrospect, one of my worst days gave me a renewed spirit for life.

All the while, I had no idea what God was going to do with me. During the divorces, suicides, single motherhood, prison, pain, shame, and suffering, he was filling me up with soulful wisdom. I found a way to be happy rather than hostile, no matter how badly life treated me.

Finding meaning in all circumstances affords you a freedom from the mental prison society often erects around us. In my first book, A Strange Path to Freedom, I share slices of the prison life through my quirky and often spiritual lens, as well as the magical moments gained from the experience. My stories offer a guide for others to free themselves from sour lemons and emotions that feel like a ball and chain. And they offer a cautionary tale for navigating ethical choices in the professional world.

Remember, the most unfathomable grief and "too much to bear" times in life can become an invitation and search for meaning. Once the mind resets and notices life differently, an ordinary cup of coffee at the kitchen table will be profound. If you can find the willingness to reflect and examine life's unbending times with humility, honesty, and a spoonful of humor, you will also create an opportunity to leave a legacy to those you love.

Whether you bask with gratitude in life's glory or fall into despair during its gloom, it's in the search for meaning that nurtures a life worth living.

## Lemonade for a Lifetime

Squeezing life's lemons into sweet lemonade is an overused statement to encourage and motivate those going through hardship and adversity. It is not a one-time event such as the death of a loved one, infidelity, infertility, loss of career, or rejection. This chaotic stage is referred to as "the fall." During these times, we feel as if we are dying in our own earthly hell as we try to return to the life we lost. But there is life on the other side of disorder after you go through it—not under, over, or around it. Like a child who kicks and screams until they tire out and rest, I wept uncontrollably until my heart broke open. I discovered this crack to be a gift—a place of union with God. It doesn't mean I've achieved a higher level of holiness, but it was a powerful entrance to a greater relationship and a confirmation that God will never forsake me.

Tears are for the soul that prepares us to see the Lord. That is why I believe it's important and humbling to "return to the well." If we don't remember the pain, how will we know the growth or remember how God touched us? It's all too easy to get sucked into a society that promotes achievement, fame, fortune, perfect bodies, and Facebook Live!

"Therefore say to them, thus declares the LORD of hosts: Return to me, says the LORD of hosts, and I will return to you, says the LORD of hosts."

ZECHARIAH 1:3

Cheers, my friend!

# Directory of Authors

**Veronica Bahn**
**Founder and CEO of Side Hustle Expert LLC./ Financial**
**Freedom Entrepreneur/ wife/ mom/ friend/ baseball mom/**
**speaker/ author/ Reiki certified/ business coach**
https://www.facebook.com/SideHustleExpert/
https://www.linkedin.com/in/veronicabahn/

**Kristine M. Binder**
**Educator, Coach, Ambassador, Advocate, and Fundraiser**
https://www.facebook.com/Tutulady22
https://linkedin.com/in/kristinebinder
tutuladykristine@gmail.com

**Lynn Brown**
**Author**
https://www.facebook.com/threethebook/
www.threethebook.com

**Aislinn Ellis**
**Professional Organizer/ Owner and Founder of AskAisi**
https://www.facebook.com/AskAisi/
https://www.askaisi.com/
https://www.linkedin.com/in/askaisi/

**Michelle M. Faust**
**Author, Blogger, Content Writer, and Podcaster**
www.lemonadelegend.com
https://www.facebook.com/LemonadeLegend/
michelle@lemonadelegend.com

**Mayra Hawkins**
**Spiritual Coach and Founder of Women Who Mean Business AZ**
https://www.facebook.com/WomanWhoMeanBusiness/
maryra@theleaptotransformation.com

**Alicia Miyares Laszewski**
**Founder of Brand Ethos**
https://www.facebook.com/yourbrandethos/
https://www.linkedin.com/company/your-brand-ethos/
alicia@yourbrandethos.com

**Davina Lyons**
**Educator, Speaker, Personal Development Coach and Founder of Tribe Authentic Woman**
https://www.facebook.com/davinalyons.thrive/
davina@tribeauthenticwoman.com

**Dr. Kristy Morgan**
**Arizona Director of Candle Wishes Foundation**
**Vice President/COO at Unity Physician Services**
https://www.facebook.com/kristy.r.morgan
kristy@candlewishes .org

**Vickie Mudra**
**CEO and Founder of the Institute for Deliberate Practice**

https://www.facebook.com/vickie.mudra
Vickie.Mudra@InstituteforDeliberatePractice.com

**Karianne Munstedt**
**Karianne Munstedt Portrait**
www.kariannemunstedt.com
kari@kariannemunstedt.com

**Tracy O'Malley**
**Founder and CEO of O'Malley Enterprises**
**Performance Coach, Enneagram Expert, Author, Speaker/**
**Founder, Strive 4 Change, LLC**
https://www.linkedin.com/in/tracy-o-malley/
https://www.facebook.com/tracy.omalley

**Holly Pasut**
**Inspirational, Motivational Speaker, Keynote Speaker, Author**
**Blogger**
https://www.facebook.com/FreedomSpeakerHolly/
https://www.linkedin.com/in/holly-pasut-b13207121/
holly@freedomspeaker.com

**Elena Porter**
**Founder of I Am 360**
www.iam360.love
https://www.facebook.com/Iam360.love/
elena@iam360.love

**Barbara Galutia Regis**
**Author, Advocate and Physician Assistant**
https://www.facebook.com/melanomahub/
https://www.facebook.com/askthepa/

**Samantha Root**
**Co-Founder of Lujo Commercial Cleaning/ Owner of Your Real Estate Group, LLC**
https://www.facebook.com/LujoCleanAZ/
https://www.facebook.com/samantha.root.3950
https://business.facebook.com/YourRealtorSamanthaRoot/

**Charlotte Shaff**
http://themediapush.com/
https://www.linkedin.com/in/themediapush/
charlotte@themediapush.com

**Kate Weeks**
**Business Development Manager at Resurrection University**
https://www.facebook.com/kate.lucking
kdaniel380@gmail.com

**Donita Bath Wheeler**
**Cancer, Life, and Survivor Coach/ Podcaster**
http://www.mamabearcancercoach.com
https://www.facebook.com/Donitamamabear/
donita@mamabearcancercoach.com

**Karen Nowicki**
**CEO of Phoenix Business RadioX**
**Creator of SoulMarks™, Deep Impact Leadership™ and MotherDaughterWeekends™**
**Speaker, Author, Coach, and Consultant**
https://businessradiox.com/phoenixbusinessradio/

# Praise for The Lemonade Stand

"The Lemonade Stand is an amazing and moving collection of stories from women who have had to endure and overcome unimaginable circumstances. The stories are inspiring and a testimony to the strength of the human spirit and determination. As the founder of DEPTH Speaking, LLC, many of the stories could be the basis for impactful, inspiring, and motivational talks."

Lauri Erickson
DEPTH Speaking

"You are not alone! The powerful stories in this book will prove that to you. In each chapter, these courageous women transparently share a time when their world turned upside down and how they turned themselves right side up again, showing up with dignity and grace. These accounts are shining examples of how you can turn lemons into lemonade."

María Tomás-Keegan
Producer & Host of Tips for the Transition
Certified Career & Life Coach for Women

"Bravo! *The Lemonade Stand* is a book for every woman who has ever faced hardship. Stories of loss, tragedy, and brokenness turned into strength, courage, and HOPE! These are stories of EVERY woman—for EVERY woman. I am left inspired and in awe of their heartfelt transparency."

Susan Ackerman
Entrepreneur and Author of *Reno Rising*

# T-shirt Order Page

Elena Porter, founder of I AM 360, created a t-shirt of a heart filled with words. These words are from all of the authors, and they represent the truth of their story. I AM 360 is on a mission to spread positive messaging around the world and to inspire change. A portion of their sales goes to charitable organizations. Porter created the Embrace Your Story t-shirt to compliment The Lemonade Stand. The book and the t-shirt make a great combination to give to a loved one as a gift. To order a T-shirt, go to www. iam360.love. You will find these T-shirts under New Arrivals.

**Lemonade Legend**
**https://www.lemonadelegend.com/**

At Lemonade Legend we provide exposure for business leaders who have a great "lemon to lemonade" story, through content writing, marketing funnels, ebooks, mini books, podcast guest experiences, media exposure, and more. Your story is your brand and we make you a legend by spotlighting you through the media channel that gives you the greatest exposure to your target market. Great content becomes the seeds of a bountiful business harvest. We take the time to personally understand you and your company's purpose, so your marketing message reflects who you are and speaks directly to your audience. We'll create powerful messaging strategies that reveal your authenticity and uniqueness. Legendary leaders are a voice, not an echo.

Contact Michelle Faust to contribute your story to the next Lemonade Legend anthology.

EMAIL: Michelle@LemonadeLegend.com
FACEBOOK: fb.com/lemonadelegend
TWITTER: @TheLemonadeSta8
INSTAGRAM: Lemonade_Legend
SPOTIFY: tinyurl.com/lemonadelegend

Made in the USA
San Bernardino, CA
11 July 2020

75402636R00163